HOW DID THIS SH*T BECOME A NUMBER 1 HIT?

FROM WTF TO #1

50 BIZARRE HITS
That Took Over the
Charts and the
Reasons Why

CABE EATON

Disclaimer: This book reflects the personal opinions, commentary, and subjective viewpoints of the author. The views expressed herein are solely those of the author and do not represent the views of any artist, songwriter, performer, record label, publisher, or any other person or entity. The inclusion of any musical work, artist, or recording in this book should not be construed as factually asserting any matter beyond the author's personal perspective and critical commentary.

Quotations of song lyrics and titles are reproduced under the fair use doctrine for the purposes of commentary, criticism, scholarship, and discussion. All copyrights in lyrics, musical compositions, sound recordings, and related works remain the property of their respective owners. No claim of ownership is made or intended by the author or publisher.

All trademarks, service marks, and trade names are the property of their respective owners and are used herein for identification, reference, and commentary purposes only. Their inclusion does not imply any sponsorship, endorsement, or affiliation with the author or this publication.

While care has been taken to provide accurate contextual information, this book is intended as opinion and commentary only, and the author and publisher disclaim any liability arising from errors, omissions, or any interpretation of the content herein.

Editing, design, and distribution by Bublish.

Published by Cabe Eaton Books

ISBN: 9798899890222 (paperback)
ISBN: 9798899890215 (eBook)

This book is dedicated to any living artist represented and/or mentioned in the following pages.

Please don't kill me.

CONTENTS

"I had a hit single on the radio for 30 days before I graduated from high school." – Will Smith

"If you can't handle the responsibility of a hit single, don't write one." – Joe Elliott (Def Leppard)

"Obviously, the hit singles get the biggest reaction. That's when you can see people really getting excited." – Kathy Valentine (the Go-Go's)

"I would be a liar if I said it wouldn't be lovely and soothing – that's the word – to have a hit single or a hit album." – Mel Tormé

"If it's on VH1, it's a hit." – Sting

Introduction

WHAT MAKES A SONG A #1 HIT?

I t's a good question. If there were a clear answer, then you, my friend, just wasted your money on this book. But in 1913, a music industry publication known as *Billboard* started ranking the most popular tunes in America. And not in a way you might imagine. These lists were compiled by using the sales figures of how many units of sheet music were sold per given song. That's right—long before stoned-out teenagers were loitering at their local record stores, they were loitering around racks stuffed with pieces of paper with musical notes peppered all over them (that is, if they didn't have something better to do). Back in those days, the term *music publishing* made far more sense because songs were primarily published on paper, much like a book, for the purpose of providing material for piano lessons, public performances, or if someone at home simply wanted to toss something onto the music stand of a dust-infested piano that had never been touched in order to impress visitors.

As the decades wore on, radio became more accessible and recorded discs had grown into mass production. Hence, by the time the 1940s came around, *Billboard* utilized record sales, radio airplay, and every single instance in which a barfly would throw a nickel into a jukebox for the data to compile their charts. After testing out different permutations of their chart listings, *Billboard* would, in 1958, create the definitive list of the most popular songs in the US: the *Billboard* Hot 100. The publication would soon ditch jukebox sales and focus this list solely on Top 40 radio airplay and the number of 45 single discs record stores could move out of their doors and onto listeners' turntables (long before listeners simply pirated the songs online, of course). The list would become an indomitable force. From Ricky Nelson's 1958 chart-topper, "Poor Little Fool," to whatever Taylor Swift happens to sneeze out onto a record, the Hot 100—the official American pop chart—continues to be the gold standard for artists as well as music industry types (or whatever is left of them) interested in getting a feel for who's hot and who's not in the business.

With such a rich history of objective data determining which singles are duds, which ones deserve that it's-moving-up-the-chart-fast bullet slapped to the left of its listing, and which few should sit cozily at the toppermost of the poppermost (as John Lennon once called it), there should be no argument against any tune that has ever reached the #1 spot.

Yeah, right. The truth is lots of questionable crap has graced the top spot of the Hot 100. In many cases, the immense popularity of an artist or the decent success of their previous single or album gave the dubious tune a bit of a boost on the chart, leaving a listener to ponder, *How did song B become a #1 hit, but song A finished outside the Top 10?*

Popularity indeed drives sales and influences radio airplay, but some #1 tunes are so dull, cringy, or flat-out batshit crazy that their rise to the top is just inexplicable. The following pages present a list of fifty such songs that have little to no excuse for their climb to the top. At the same time, this author will do his best to conjure possible reasons as to why the tunes became top hits by means of historical context, pop culture, or good old-fashioned educated guesses.

This list will try to avoid #1 hits that, as mentioned above, were the result of an artist's momentum, but with exceptions given to those hits that are completely confounding and ridiculous. Posthumous releases will also be given a pass. We will also ignore unworthy chart-toppers that achieved their peak status due to the success of a blockbuster film ("Batdance," "The Candy Man") or those that were derived from some moronic trend ("Convoy," "The Streak").

In addition, any tune that had coasted along on the coattails of a music scene will be spared from embarrassment. This includes chart-topping drivel like Herman's Hermits' "I'm Henry VIII, I Am" or "Disco Duck" by Rick Dees and His Cast of Idiots. (He said it, not me.) Most bubblegum hits will also be excluded, as even the brats enjoy listening to records.

This list will focus heavily on the time frame ranging from the early 1960s through the early 1990s, as it was during this time span that *Billboard* pulled airplay data exclusively from Top 40 radio, which was comprised of multiple music genres. Single-record sales had also petered out by the 1980s, causing some uncertainty when it came to record sales data. Today's popularity of downloads and streaming services does give *Billboard* ample data to work from, although virtually all radio station formats now contribute to the airplay data, which tends to skew the results. And considering how pallid a lot of hit music has been during the past couple of decades, putting down many chart-toppers today would be as easy as putting down *Sharknado*. Nevertheless, hits from the past few decades are included in the list since, even though the rules have changed and more recent tunes might not be everyone's cup of tea, oddballs are oddballs and deserve to be called out.

Another thing worth mentioning is that yours truly is a fan of some of the tunes about to be discussed and/or obliterated. The piles of vinyl records, CDs, and cassette tapes that have accumulated in my collection for decades did so for a reason (aside from the purpose of filling in the corners of my bedroom). So, yes, *shit* would be a misnomer in such instances. But being an admirer of a song does not mean the song itself should have been the hottest hit in the country. Even the nuttiest psychopath who listens to Lou Reed's *Metal Machine Music* on repeat must know that none of those tracks should be anywhere near the top of any chart.

And finally, the Hot 100 is purely an American chart. So, if you're somewhere in the middle of Pakistan reading this book, you might have no clue about any song or artist that will soon be discussed. But I appreciate your business.

So sit back and enjoy the book. It is highly recommended you check the songs out for yourself before poring through the chapters. After which, feel free to agree or disagree with any (or all) of the selections included, as they are just based on one guy's opinion. But I trust you will agree that most of these picks aren't worthy of the very sheet music *Billboard* used to tally sales over a hundred years ago in order to let America know what songs were the bee's knees and which ones deserved to 23-skidoo their way out of the public's fickle attention span.

Now, on with the shit.

LARRY VERNE—"MR. CUSTER" (1960)

Novelty songs have certainly been a part of *Billboard*'s nascent days of the Hot 100. By the end of 1958, "The Chipmunk Song (Christmas Don't Be Late)" was annoying the yuletide hell out of everybody yet still managed to top the chart. But in October of 1960, Larry Verne's rise to top, via the god-awful novelty hit "Mr. Custer," could very well be the eighth wonder of the world.

This author has no intention of excoriating *Billboard* for rewarding any past work deemed too politically incorrect for today's standards. We all know the mention of "injuns" and "redskins"—as well as some hand-over-the-mouth war whoops—would unequivocally earn "Mr. Custer" a lifetime ban from any kind of office-friendly playlist. But what is considered offensive these days may not have been the case over sixty years ago, which means the objectionable content alone wouldn't have prevented the song's ascension on the Hot 100. And this author has no interest in seeking out tunes of a politically incorrect flair to expose them in this book. If that were the case, Carl Douglas's 1974 chart-topping trend chaser "Kung Fu Fighting" would find a nice, cozy home on the list.

Regardless, *as* a song, "Mr. Custer" is downright horrible. In it, Verne delivers a plea to General George Custer—by means of a sickly hillbilly dialect—not to send him with the cavalry to the fateful Battle of the Little Bighorn. The slow, droning march does Verne no favors in the rhythm department as he obnoxiously whines, "Puuleeese, Mister Custer, ah do' wanna go!" The song slightly redeems itself, comedically, when the narrator's buddy Charlie gets impaled in the head. (Well, it's funnier on the recording than how it reads here.) But when Verne later tries to search for the "injun word for friend" and comes up with "Kemosabe" from *The Lone Ranger*, the annoyance comes roaring back and all you want to do at this point is shoot Verne in the face with an arrow to shut him up.

What on earth could have caused "Mr. Custer" to escalate to the top of the Hot 100? Were people bored doing "The Twist"? Were listeners too distracted by the beads of sweat running down Richard Nixon's face during his debate with John F. Kennedy to bother looking for anything good on the radio or finding any decent records to purchase at Woolworth? Perhaps the inane nature of "Mr. Custer" was part of some kind of ongoing trend on the charts. BULL'S-EYE!

As mentioned above, novelty songs were a veritable force during the early years of the *Billboard* Hot 100. Just two short months before "Mr. Custer" had risen to the top of the chart, Bryan Hyland had scored a chart-topper of his own with "Itsy Bitsy Teenie Weenie Yellow Polka Dot Bikini." The goofball summer anthem peaked at #1 in August 1960, right before all the teenyboppers had to pack up their sunscreen and beach balls to face a new school year. But just a month before string bikinis were the thingy on the Hot 100, the Hollywood Argyles would score a #1 hit with the comic strip–inspired "Alley Oop." Hence, "Mr. Custer" simply could have served as the final installment in a triad of twaddle before being put out of its misery after just a week of chart domination. Whatever the reason may be with the rise and fall of "Mr. Custer," things were about to get a lot kookier on the charts.

THE TORNADOS—"TELSTAR" (1962)

"**T**elstar"—named after the telecommunications satellite launched in 1962—is a revolutionary instrumental piece. Recorded by British quintet the Tornados (*sic*), the tune is musically centered around a clavioline, the primitive keyboard responsible for the warped, spiraling sound heard throughout the track, giving the piece a sci-fi attribute. The song's catchy "rah-rah" melody sounds like a pep rally tune a high school marching band might toot out of their cheap instruments after the home football team manages to stumble into the end zone. "Telstar" is indeed cool and interesting, yet it sounds more like a bizarre science project as opposed to a song. And this science project puzzlingly managed to get launched all the way to the top of the Hot 100 during the final two weeks of 1962.

The Tornados weren't so much a traditional band but rather a performing vehicle that producer-songwriter Joe Meek utilized to record his musical concoctions. And Meek was nothing less than mentally unhinged, as evidenced by his throwing of a towering recording machine downstairs at one of the band members or screaming at producer Phil Spector on the phone while accusing him of stealing his sounds. (And if Phil Spector thought you were nuts, you were *nuts*.) But Meek hit the jackpot with the Tornados' recording of "Telstar," which would earn for the quintet the honor of being the first British rock ensemble to hit #1 in the US. (You heard that right—it *wasn't* the Beatles.) Meek would spend much of the '60s using the Tornados to record his songs. If any member would spin off into the sunset, the hot-headed producer would simply replace him, à la Menudo. This process would continue until the band's hits began to dry up, and it would come to a permanent halt in 1967, after Meek blasted most of his head off with the very shotgun he had just murdered his landlady with.

Now that this author is out of danger from Meek's psychotic rage, it's safe to say that "Telstar" has the hit potential of a batboy. As innovative as the track is, what exactly were listeners shaking their asses to? The melody is rich, but the slow, quarter-note pattern is reminiscent of something built into a cheap Casio keyboard, challenging the novice player to match note for note before rewarding the beginner with a patronizing "good job, kiddo" sound effect.

It wasn't unusual for an instrumental track to top the Hot 100, as Dave "Baby" Cortez grazed the #1 spot for one week in May 1959 with the sock-hop instrumental "The Happy Organ." Of course, the Edgar Winter Group would later do the same for one week in May 1973 with "Frankenstein," an ass-kicking instrumental that implemented plenty of happy keyboard instruments. But not only did "Telstar" top the chart, its reign lasted from December 22, 1962, until January 5 of the following year. What the hell?

Here's a theory: Just after the world nearly ended in October 1962 via the Cuban Missile Crisis, the Hot 100 became a little corny. The Crystals' bad-ass-boyfriend anthem, "He's a Rebel," crept up to the top of the chart for a couple of weeks, followed by the Four Seasons' "Big Girls Don't Cry," which stayed put at the top for a whopping five weeks. An apocalypse-weary America, annoyed with all that falsetto whining that continued well into the Thanksgiving weekend, was ready for a break. With the holi-day season in full force, some Christmas cheer was surely in order. Hence, Americans could very well have confused "Telstar" for a Christmas song, sans any yuletide lyrics or sleigh bells.

Before you laugh at this theory, just know that something quite insane happened right after the November 1963 John F. Kennedy assassination. The Singing Nun's "Dominique"—a silly song this author will leave off the list due to its endur-ing absurdity and possible Kennedy/Catholicism connection—dominated the Hot 100 during the entire month of December. And while the instrumental "Telstar" contained no words, "Dominique" was sung entirely in French, leaving a vast major-ity of Americans oblivious to what was being sung; all they knew was that someone wearing a habit was goofily singing it. If this author's Christmas theory is correct about "Telstar," that sister certainly did her homework twelve months later.

LORNE GREENE—"RINGO" (1964)

When all else fails, just confuse listeners into buying your record.

Bonanza was without question one of the most beloved and successful TV shows in American history. Running from 1959 until 1973, *Bonanza* saw four presidential administrations, one war, and more than its share of nauseating fashion trends. And it wasn't easy for a Western to stand out amid an overabundance of programs featuring six-shooters and dramatic horse chases beneath anachronistic jet streaks in the sky. But America became well acquainted with the Cartwrights, and Canadian actor Lorne Greene would become one of the most recognizable TV dads (well, a TV dad that didn't look much older than two of his three TV sons).

Greene was so well known that during the early '60s, RCA Records thought it would be a good idea to sign the actor to a record deal for the purpose of exploiting *Bonanza* and every fake square inch of the Ponderosa Ranch. After the release of a few silly long-players called *Bonanza Ponderosa Party Time* and *Christmas on the Ponderosa,* Greene and RCA struck gold with the 1964 album *Welcome to the Ponderosa*. The album would edge into the Top 40, thanks to a song called "Ringo."

There's nothing very spectacular about "Ringo." The song is structured with a boom-chicka-boom rhythm one might hear on a Johnny Cash record. Greene provides a spoken-word vocal of the titular outlaw, who spares the life of a sheriff who had previously nursed him back to health, only to be turned into Swiss cheese by the sheriff's posse. As Greene's recitation grows more intense with the ascending chord changes, a group of baritone singers sporadically chant, "Rin-goooooo."

The tune would peak at the top of the Hot 100 for one week in December 1964, causing plenty of bewilderment among followers of pop music, as well as a lot of suspicion among others that the similarity between the song's title character and a certain mop-topped drummer had everything to do with its enormous success.

The fact is 1964 belonged to the Beatles. Therefore, it wouldn't be completely out of line to suggest that a few shenanigans at the record stores could have helped push "Ringo" straight to the top of the charts. For example, let's suppose Betty Lou is invited to Betty Sue's birthday party and asks her mother to pick up something by the Beatles for a gift. Mom soon finds herself wandering aimlessly inside a record store and randomly picks up a record with "Ringo" printed on the cover. Since the store is short on actual Beatles merchandise, the cashier clams up and sells the poor woman something Betty Sue wouldn't be caught dead with: a dreamy picture of Lorne Greene on an album cover. On the day of the party, humiliation ensues.

This alleged Beatles-related conspiracy is somewhat plausible, but there would have to be lots and lots of ill-fated birthday parties for "Ringo" to sell enough copies to achieve its climb to the top. And Lord knows, radio airplay couldn't have caused any Beatles/*Bonanza* ambiguation. Simply put, "Ringo" was an anomaly in the history of the Hot 100.

Or was it?

HOW DID THIS SH*T BECOME A NUMBER 1 HIT?

In 1977, actor David Soul—who played the latter role on *Starsky & Hutch*—would score his own chart-topper with "Don't Give Up on Us," an accomplishment that would last for one week in April of that year. And this week was wedged in between the chart-topping success of two disco-drenched hits: ABBA's "Dancing Queen" and Thelma Houston's "Don't Leave Me This Way." So maybe—just maybe—the world stops every now and then to take note when an ephemeral TV star tries his hand at making records.

GARY LEWIS AND THE PLAYBOYS—
"THIS DIAMOND RING" (1965)

During the mid-1960s, pop music's best-kept secret involved a group of LA session men and women known as the Wrecking Crew. Made up of superb musicians like drummer Hal Blaine, guitarist Tommy Tedesco, and bassist Carol Kaye, these players provided the music for numerous hit records, including those by the Beach Boys, the Monkees, and the Grass Roots. And record consumers were none the wiser.

Meanwhile, in New York, keyboardist Al Kooper— who would soon be heard on Bob Dylan's landmark 1965 LP, *Highway 61 Revisited*—was a struggling songwriter who, along with Bob Brass and Irwin Levine, had come up with a zinger of a tune called "This Diamond Ring." The melodious, multikey composition was designed for an R&B ensemble to tackle. But when the Drifters turned it down, the tune got a bit whiter after being presented to heartthrob crooner Bobby Vee. After Vee passed on the offer, the song got even whiter and exceptionally nerdy when given to Disneyland house band Gary and the Playboys by LA producer Snuff Garrett. Backed by members of the Wrecking Crew, "This Diamond Ring" was on its way to the top.

Singer and drummer Gary Lewis—the son of comedian Jerry Lewis—and his Playboy buddies only had to compete with a simultaneous release of "This Diamond Ring" by R&B vocalist Sammy Ambrose during the early weeks of 1965. But Ambrose's version soon fizzled off the charts, as America seemed to fall in love with Lewis's nasally reading of the soul-intended piece. By February, the rechristened Gary *Lewis* and the Playboys—who barely, if at all, participated on the track itself—became a bona fide overnight sensation with a #1 pop hit to their expanded name.

It's likely that the Jerry Lewis connection had something to do with the chart success of the actor and comedian's son. The Martin & Lewis days were long gone, but Jerry was still a force to be reckoned with on the silver screen via the 1963 blockbuster flick *The Nutty Professor*.

Still, who gives a damn about a geek and his bling?

The consummately arranged backing track for "This Diamond Ring" is apparent to the ears, but even former Wrecking-Crew-member-turned-piano-rock-icon Leon Russell—who played on and arranged the track—later reminisced on the 2015 documentary *The Wrecking Crew!*, "When we cut that record, I said 'Oh my God, I hate this shit.'" This is ironic, being that Russell's dainty piano tinkles, which connect the choruses back to the verses, are the musical highlights of the recording that effectively hold the elements of the track together. Garrett's fine production value certainly didn't hurt the song's commercial viability, but still—this ring deserves a nice little trip down a drainpipe.

By 1965, the Beatles had by no means faded into obscurity. Hence, all attempts were made by US record companies to either sign or manufacture all-American rock acts to give the Fab Four a run for their millions. And when teenyboppers in the US had worn out their Beatles 45s and long-players, they would occasionally drop into the record stores to buy a product made in the USA. But why "This Diamond Ring"? WHY?

Sure, I'm giving Gary Lewis and the Playboys a hard time, but the truth is the group put out far better subsequent records (however much they musically contributed to them). Their two follow-up singles, "Count Me In" and "Save Your Heart for Me," from an aesthetic perspective, run circles around "This Diamond Ring," yet both hits stalled at #2 on the Hot 100. Adding insult to injury, "Count Me In" was kept from the top of the chart by Herman's Hermits' barf bag of a single "Mrs. Brown, You've Got a Lovely Daughter." And *that* just might be the real explanation: "This Diamond Ring" was merely a rest stop before teenyboppers fled right back to those funny-talking hitmakers from across the pond.

Works for me.

THE McCOYS—"HANG ON SLOOPY" (1965)

During the late '80s, an oldies album compilation simply known as *Fun Rock* aired on repeat during commercial breaks for *St. Elsewhere*, *Who's the Boss?* and such. This compilation set, which was offered on either four records or three giant cassettes (as opposed to tiny ones), advertised pure, cheesy fun for both the ears and the hips. The material on *Fun Rock* was deemed as "songs your body can't resist." Actors dressed as construction workers, cops, grocery shoppers, and waitresses (and no—these weren't the Village People) can be seen in the commercial rocking out and lip-syncing to crusty classics like "Blue Moon," "Splish Splash," and "Wild Thing."

One clip in the commercial particularly drew my attention as a kid. It showed two actors decked out as a doctor and nurse flanking another actor dressed in a hospital gown. The latter is a sad sight, but the two professionals encourage the poor bastard by lip-syncing, "Hang on, Snoopy, Snoopy hang on!" Or so I thought. The cartoon beagle is nowhere to be found in the brief clip, but what *did* happen to Snoopy? Was he on his deathbed behind the three actors? Was the guy in the gown supposed to be Snoopy (assuming there was a copyright infringement issue preventing the famous dog to be shown)?

Sure, I might have been a dopey eleven-year-old, but—mostly after paying attention to the title of the song flashing below the actors—I finally realized the character in the song was not so much the *Peanuts* character but rather a person called "Sloopy." The infectious groove that encapsulates the song—shamelessly borrowed from that of "Louie, Louie"—is only matched by the frat-house chant of the chorus. The track arguably has all the fixings of a hit single. There's just one question: WHAT THE HELL IS A "SLOOPY"?

"Hang on Sloopy" has a history involving multiple artists getting their grubby paws all over it. After an R&B outfit called the Vibrations took the song (originally entitled "My Girl Sloopy") into the Top 40 in 1964, a faux rock band called the Strangeloves (comprised of record producers) planned on recording the tune themselves but didn't want to put the single out while their current single, 1965's "I Want Candy," was doing some damage of its own on the Hot 100. The Strangeloves would relinquish the tune to British invaders the Dave Clark Five before coming across an Ohio-based teenage band called Rick and the Raiders (whose leader, Rick Derringer, would later record the 1973 hit "Rock and Roll, Hoochie Koo"). Bringing the boys to New York, the Strangeloves would record the youngsters' vocals over a prerecorded track, change the ensemble's name to the McCoys, and provide them with a solid #1 hit in October 1965.

It's more than obvious Sloopy is a female love interest of the song's narrator. And it wasn't unusual for male purveyors of hit songs to use idiotic names to describe their girlfriends (see "Bony Moronie"). But I cannot get past the whole "Sloopy" thing. It just doesn't roll off the tongue. In fact, an odd slurring sound is made when the word is said, which totally explains why there were never any hit songs with titles such as "Slick and Slimy Bastards," "Super-Sleuths on Ski Slopes," or "Slip Slidin' Away" (bad example).

One theory behind the song's chart-topping success—aside from the possible misunderstanding of the name of the title character—might have something to do with another weirdly titled song from 1965. Just before the summer of that year, a wily band from Dallas by the name of Sam the Sham and the Pharaohs had a smoking-hot, fratty single called "Wooly Bully," which reached #2 on the Hot 100. It failed to knock both "Help Me, Rhonda" by the Beach Boys and "Back in My Arms Again" by the Supremes off the top spot. So Sloopy's ascension to the top could very well have matched the same trajectory as "Wooly Bully," only the McCoys didn't have the Beach Boys or the Supremes to ward off during their song's one-week run in October.

Of course, "Hang on Sloopy," to this day, has plenty of staying power. More than a handful of artists have since recorded their own versions of the rocker (with varying degrees of success), and Ohio State University's marching band still uses it as their signature rally song. (Could that weird mascot that's supposed to be a buckeye instead be a Sloopy?)

One thing for sure is the subject of the tune has nothing to do with the cartoon beagle. And as for the *Fun Rock* commercial, the goofy actors could very well be shaking their stethoscopes to "Sloopy," "Snoopy," "Droopy," or even "Poopy." It didn't matter. It was all about having fun and giving one's body a song it just could not resist. And perhaps the need to make the most of beer-fueled frat house toga parties gave "Hang on Sloopy" a major nudge to its brief status as a #1 hit. For now, Snoopy is safe and sound.

6

SSGT. BARRY SADLER—
"THE BALLAD OF THE GREEN BERETS" (1966)

This chapter is in no way intended to besmirch, belittle, or berate the late Barry Sadler or his service to his country. Sadler's patriotism has been well displayed and well documented. But no one gets a free pass when it comes to putting out shitty music.

Staff Sergeant Barry Sadler served as a medic in the Vietnam War before being sidelined in 1965 after suffering a severe leg injury by means of a punji stick that was set up as a booby trap. While recovering, Sadler, who dabbled in songwriting, composed an excruciatingly lengthy ode in honor of the US Army Green Beret branch that he was part of. Robin Moore, who penned the 1965 book *The Green Berets*, got ahold of the song and edited it down to something that he thought just might have a chance on the Hot 100. And despite a non-pop-friendly military snare drum cadence, corny lyrics, and a vocal performance that would make "Yankee Doodle" seem hip and suave, Moore was right. "The Ballad of the Green Berets," released on the RCA Victor label, would spend a mind-boggling total of five weeks at the top of the Hot 100 in the spring of 1966.

The outdated arrangement and overall sound of the recording itself seem out of place enough for 1966. But Sadler immediately throws us a forkball in the first verse as he describes the Special Forces group in the title as those who "jump and die." Jump and die? JUMP AND DIE? Did Sadler and Moore forget to revisit that lyric? Sadler makes the men sound like salmon jumping into the mouths of grizzly bears. As the song continues, the lyrics aren't as bad, but six verses—including one that repeats—are a little tough to take (believe it or not, the song was originally composed with *twelve* verses). Amazingly, the track spans less than two and a half minutes.

(I mean, instead of "jump and die," couldn't the lyric have been "fight and die" or "give their lives"? Sure, I'm no Tim Rice, but it's just a suggestion.)

The chart run of "The Ballad of the Green Berets" is somewhat easy to ascertain. In September of 1965, Barry McGuire took the apocalyptic anti-war anthem "Eve of Destruction" to the top of the Hot 100 for one week. (Funnily enough, "Hang on Sloopy" dethroned the single from the top the following week.) Augmented by the ongoing counterculture movement, "Eve of Destruction" was bound to attract a response from the silent majority, and it came in the form of Sadler's tune. But five weeks at the top is a little hard to explain.

(Didn't someone at RCA Victor notice the "jump and die" lyric before the vinyl was pressed and at least try to alert somebody?)

Yes, the silent majority—riveted by Lyndon B. Johnson's hyperbolic 1964 Daisy Ad and who weren't yet turned off by the carnage of the Vietnam War by the mid-1960s—bought records and even bothered to make requests on the radio every now and then. But how did the song hold up for five consecutive weeks? The answer might be staring us right smack-dab in the face: People simply loved the song and sympathized with its narrator.

(Am I the only one who thinks the "jump and die" lyric is weird?)

Not only did "The Ballad of the Green Berets" sell over nine million copies as a single, but it inspired the 1968 John Wayne flick *The Green Berets*, which was based on Moore's book and undoubtedly green-lighted by the song. Over the years, the song would find itself being both celebrated and parodied in films and TV shows alike, whether it be *Caddyshack* or *Cheers*. So "The Ballad of the Green Berets" obviously made an impact on people who either admired the very men Sadler sang so proudly of or wondered in disbelief during the entire month of March 1966, "How did this shit become a #1 hit?"

7

THE BEATLES—"PAPERBACK WRITER" (1966)

Just hold your fire and hear me out on this one.

This chapter could easily be the most controversial entry in this book. To criticize any chart-topper by the Fab Four would be considered sacrilege by any Beatles fan who shelled out a couple Hamiltons for the "Now and Then" single on vinyl. And yes, yours truly is bending the rules slightly when it comes to attacking a song that topped the Hot 100 while the given artist was on fire. And the Beatles were indeed still smoldering by 1966. But what's the deal with "Paperback Writer," the most forgettable 45 A-side issued by the mop-topped quartet?

The Beatles—namely head songwriters John Lennon and Paul McCartney—knew exactly what they were doing when crafting pop records. Just listen to the group's first US chart-topper, "I Want to Hold Your Hand." The loud opening first bar that kicks off a commotion of rhythm and chords supporting otherwise mushy lyrics was completely by design. Now listen to "Paperback Writer." The multilayered a cappella tagline sung by Lennon, McCartney, and George Harrison is beyond impressive, but the song continues with a modest guitar pattern backed by two chords, a steady beat, and a blundered group vocal at the final verse (which might just be a bad edit). Even Lennon later noted in *Playboy* the tune "is son of 'Day Tripper' (the band's December 1965 single), meaning a rock and roll song with a guitar lick on a fuzzy, loud guitar." Musically, the composition is so basic that the focus is on McCartney's lead vocal, which describes the exciting adventures of a bootlicking novelist looking for a break.

"Paperback Writer" should have fallen off the Hot 100 before it approached anywhere near the top spot, which it had captured for two nonconsecutive weeks in June and July of 1966. During the year 1965, every new single the Beatles had issued in America became a #1 hit. The band was so hot by the end of the year that even when their US label, Capitol Records, watered down their groundbreaking December LP, *Rubber Soul*, by swapping tunes in and out of it as if it were a mixtape, American kids still rushed out to get it, as well as the simultaneously issued "We Can Work It Out/Day Tripper" double A-sided single.

As Capitol was taking liberties with the *Rubber Soul* track listing, they stripped the Byrds-like "Nowhere Man" off the set, intending to release it as a stand-alone single in the US in February 1966 before slapping it on the infamous butcher-decorated *Yesterday and Today* compilation LP, released four months later. After its February release, the single would peak at #3 on the Hot 100 before heading off into its nowhere land. The Beatles' #1 streak in the US was over, and it wouldn't be until four months later that another product by the group would show up in record stores . . . Guess what product that was?

"Paperback Writer" is by no means a horrible song. But when you look at some of its chart-topping predecessors— including the folksy "Monday, Monday" by the Mamas and the Papas and the Rolling Stones' sulky rocker "Paint It, Black"—it's surprising that a song about a loser trying to sell his dumb book to a publisher (ahem) would get chosen as the next Beatles single. The tune's B-side, the trippy-hippy "Rain," would have been a much better fit for such colorful times.

The one conclusion I could come up with for the two-week run of "Paperback Writer" on top of the Hot 100—aside from the fact that listeners were sick to death of "The Ballad of the Green Berets"—is that Beatles fans weren't completely blown away by the February 1966 release of "Nowhere Man" (which was never intended as a single by the Fab Four anyway), and the pure hype of an upbeat number compelled radio stations to play the 45 on repeat, thus drawing kids in the millions to the record stores. (When you take away Coca-Cola, people get antsy.) But today, if you ask any typical Beatles fan what the group's top five tunes are, rarely will you find "Paperback Writer" anywhere on the list. It's just not a fab track.

As for the song's nonconsecutive two-week run on the top of the Hot 100, the single that had dethroned "Paperback Writer" from the top spot during the interim week was "Strangers in the Night" by Frank Sinatra. Therefore, it's possible the pop world found the Ol' Blue Eyes standard far too doo-by-dooby dull to last very long at the top and, purely by default, "Paperback Writer" roared right back up to #1. Whatever the case might have been, a month after the commercial peak of "Paperback Writer," Capitol Records released the Beatles' songs "Eleanor Rigby" and "Yellow Submarine" as a double A-side single—as they did in 1965 with the "We Can Work It Out/Day Tripper" 45 disc—but neither tune would succeed in topping the Hot 100. After which, the Fab Four would drop out of music and resort to bagging groceries at a corner store in Liverpool. (Just making sure I haven't lost you yet.)

8

THE NEW VAUDEVILLE BAND— "WINCHESTER CATHEDRAL" (1966)

There is shit and there is *total* shit. The New Vaudeville Band's (mostly) instrumental chart-topper, "Winchester Cathedral," without question fits in the latter category. 1966 was an epic year for #1 hits, whether it be the Lovin' Spoonful's "Summer in the City," the Four Tops' "Reach Out I'll Be There," or the aforementioned "Paint It, Black" by the Rolling Stones. Why exactly a tune that could very well have been extracted from a Laurel and Hardy short found itself at the top of the Hot 100—and for three friggin' weeks—is a tough one to figure out.

Much like the Strangeloves, the New Vaudeville Band was an artificial concoction. British producer Geoff Stephens formed the "band" as an early-twentieth-century throwback to maestros of tacky music only a flapper-chasing fool would be able to groove out to. Since certain British Invasion acts (namely, the Kinks) were dabbling in old music hall stylings for some of their records, why not go all in with fancy three-piece suits and rusty instruments one might find buried underneath the clutter of a high school band room.

The whistle-led melody that drives the first part of "Winchester Cathedral" is atrocious enough, but when the lead vocal arrives, the real trouble begins. A session singer by the name of John Carter cups his hand around his mouth to make his vocal sound as if it's blowing out of a megaphone. And just when you think things couldn't get any worse, it soon becomes apparent that the lyrics level the blame toward a nine-hundred-year-old church for merely standing still while the narrator's honey gets away. You read that correctly, folks, a *church*. Not even a few fuzz guitar riffs could add any element of coolness to this track. Somewhere, a frustrated Lawrence Welk must have been screaming, "Damn it, why can't *I* score a chart-topper with crap like this?"

There is certainly an über-English flair to the New Vaudeville Band and their dreadful song, although, ironically, the tune would get only as far as #4 on the pop charts across the pond. Perhaps most Brits thought any dude who would blame the Winchester Cathedral for his own failure to commit was probably very, very pissed (drunk, that is, to us Yanks).

The only thing that could make one hate "Winchester Cathedral" any more is if it handed out a jury duty summons. But some force of nature obviously caused the song to reach the top of the Hot 100 in December 1966. True, "You're a Mean One, Mr. Grinch" didn't have a snowball's chance in hell of topping the charts, but there's no way anyone in their right mind could have confused "Winchester Cathedral" with a Christmas carol. This author is officially stumped and concludes that everybody's brain must have fallen out of their heads by the end of the year—it's the only logical explanation. Just kidding.

Much like listeners enjoyed musical acts dressed up in musty military garb, ready at any minute to fire a musket at an innocent oak tree (see Paul Revere and the Raiders, Gary Puckett and the Union Gap), they were surely accepting of a gimmick that involved fashions and music that at least postdated the Teddy Roosevelt administration. "Winchester Cathedral" was simply a flash that made a big splash in the pan. And in essence, the New Vaudeville Band owned the music hall genre of the Swinging Sixties. (But frankly, who the hell else would want to?)

Indeed, "Winchester Cathedral" can be written off as another flash in the pan, but wait . . . there's more! After the tune had occupied the top of the Hot 100 during the first week of December 1966, the Beach Boys' innovative (and extraordinarily expensive) single "Good Vibrations" took over the #1 placement during the second week, only to lose the spot to the recurring nightmare known as "Winchester Cathedral" for two more miserable weeks. Mercifully, the Monkees would come to the rescue at the final week of December to fill the top spot with "I'm a Believer," holding the #1 position strong for the first six weeks of 1967.

The New Vaudeville Band's hard-to-kill single was finally put to death on the charts by the end of 1966. But the tune would ultimately have the last laugh at the 1967 Grammys ceremony, picking up the award for Best Contemporary Rock and Roll Recording. And you cannot blame an old building for that.

BOBBY GOLDSBORO—"HONEY" (1968)

Married With Children patriarch Al Bundy had once described Bobby Goldsboro's 1968 chart-topper, "Honey," as a "musical sphincter lock." That might be too kind. Syrupy tunes about dead loved ones are always good attention-getters for sentimental suckers. And a heartstring-puller written about a widower who laments for his deceased wife certainly has the "cha-ching" formula for chart success. But when the widower describes his lost lover as a dumb klutz who likes to wreck cars, the wistfulness is lost rather quickly.

"Honey" was penned by country songwriter Bobby Russell for Bob Shane—one third of the Kingston Trio—to record in early 1968. Shane's version wouldn't attract too many greenback dollars, so vocalist Bobby Goldsboro, whose biggest hit up to that point was the 1963 Top 10 single "See the Funny Little Clown," would take a crack at the tune. (It couldn't be worse than the singer's 1964 recording of the Bacharach-David vomit-inducer, "Me Japanese Boy I Love You," right?) Goldsboro's effort would pay off, as his version of "Honey" would top the country chart and rise to the #1 spot on the Hot 100 for five straight weeks in March 1968. The tune's chart reign would follow a four-week run at the top by the posthumous Otis Redding single, "(Sittin' On) The Dock of the Bay," and precede a two-week run at the top by Archie Bell and the Drells' funk-tastic hit, "Tighten Up." "Honey" was a smash hit throughout much of the world, outselling 1968 chart-toppers like the Doors' "Hello, I Love You" and the Beatles' "Hey Jude," which topped the Hot 100 for nine weeks during the fall. The world wanted a sad song and it surely got one with "Honey." But good grief.

The saga of "Honey" begins with the narrating widower—as represented by Goldsboro—sitting in front of a tree that was planted before his wife's passing. He reminisces of his wife running into the house after tending to the tree, only to slip and nearly suffer a serious injury much to his laughing amusement. But after the widower refers to his wife as being "kinda dumb," most reasonable listeners would stop and ask themselves, "Did he really just say that?" Barry Sadler's "jump and die" lyric has nothing on this insanity (and it's at this point that Honey probably regrets sliding into her husband's DMs in the first place). The wife then wrecks the family car and fears the wrath of her husband (that is, if he's finished laughing at her falling on her ass). Without giving any specifics, the widower, in the fourth verse, describes the day his wife was taken by the angels; this could explain the ghostly female howls heard throughout the track. And just when you think the song is over, Goldsboro goes right back into the first verse before the music fades out, as if the song itself is annoyed and decides to just give up.

A cringeworthy recording like "Honey" could easily have fit in with the pop world a decade before the tune's 1968 release. It's feasible to see Goldsboro hobnobbing with the likes of Bobby Darin or Conway Twitty, as schmaltz was certainly in style back in the late '50s. But for such a turbulent year that provided rockers like "Born to Be Wild," "White Room," and "Piece of My Heart," why was so much attention—*five* straight weeks of attention (!)—paid to a tune that could very well find a loving home on the Lifetime channel? Supposedly, listeners needed a break from the rambunctious and tie-dyed tunes that were splashed all over the radio and even tolerated a ballad narrated by an insensitive creep to achieve that respite.

Interestingly, Bobby Goldsboro would strike back on the pop charts with the 1970 Mac Davis–penned "Watching Scotty Grow," which is another syrupy ode, this time directed toward a son who evidently has a learning disorder. The single would get as far as the #11 spot on the Hot 100 in February 1971 but fail to achieve the #1 status that "Honey" achieved three years earlier. The public's heartstrings were just a little too hard for the singer to tug on by the early '70s.

JEANNIE C. RILEY—
"HARPER VALLEY P.T.A." (1968)

O h, where to begin with this one.
First off, here's a synopsis of "Harper Valley P.T.A.": Girl comes home from Harper Valley Junior High with a note in her hand from the secretary of the PTA. The note is addressed to her mother, spelling out how much of a scantily clad, drunken skank she is and that they're concerned about the influence she is having on her daughter. The outraged mother then shows up to the next PTA meeting in her miniskirt calling out all the members as hypocrites who booze it up and sleep around themselves. (She's a supercool mom, anyway.)

"Harper Valley P.T.A." was written by renowned country singer-songwriter Tom T. Hall. Before Hall sung of his affinity for beer and baby ducks during the '70s, he penned this 1968 hit that topped both the pop and country charts for Jeannie C. Riley, who would become the first female artist to do so. Interestingly, Riley wasn't the first candidate to take on "Harper Valley P.T.A.," as the song was originally intended for and recorded by Margie Singleton. The singer nudged Hall into composing a tune in the same vein as that of the tragic "Ode to Billy Joe," a #1 hit for Bobbie Gentry in 1967. Instead, Riley—a secretary for country artist Jerry Chesnut—recorded the more popular version that hit the top of the Hot 100.

Riley was a secretary. Singleton was an established recording artist. Something doesn't add up here.

As far as the content of the song itself, timing could have worked in its favor, as the tune claimed the #1 spot just a couple of weeks after the September 7, 1968, Miss America pageant protest took place. A tale of a shamed woman looking for vindication could easily have gone over well with the women's liberation crowd. But if Hall wore a bra, I seriously doubt he would have burned it. (Sweet dreams with that visual, by the way.) And if he possessed the proclivity to do so, there's no way the tune would have gotten very far on the country side of the musical spectrum, where the stars still had shaven faces and pressed outfits.

And let's examine the storyline. It's not entirely clear if the daughter herself is dressed up in a miniskirt, only that she brings a note home intended for her mother from the PTA. Personally, as someone who witnessed many friends get sent home from high school for wearing Big Johnson T-shirts, I think it would have been so much better if the song started off with the girl being sent home for her own freaky threads, drawing the ire of Mom. In contrast, the PTA is merely using the student to pass a note. And this brings up the question: Did PTA groups have their own offices on school campuses back in the '60s? And did they exist only for the purpose of writing nasty notes to renegade parents, using their children as homing pigeons?

One thing that's quite noticeable when listening to "Harper Valley P.T.A."—aside from the admittedly clever twist uncovered at the end during which we learn the narrator is the daughter—is that the tune was not only inspired by the aforementioned "Ode to Billy Joe," but musically, it's a clone of the latter (with lyrics that aren't quite as disturbing). Hence, one can imagine a lot of people listening to "Harper Valley P.T.A." for the first time and asking themselves, "Didn't I hear this one last year?" Yes, copycat songs can sell, too.

"Harper Valley P.T.A." resided at the top of the Hot 100 for one week in September before the Beatles wiped out most of the fall with "Hey Jude," so it's easy to write off Riley's hit as a "Harper Valley U.F.O." But over a decade after its brief tenure at the top of the chart, both a film and a TV series spawned from the song. It obviously dressed to impress.

The longevity of "Harper Valley P.T.A."—whether on the big screen, the small screen, or as a platter—is indeed a bit of a mystery. But as long as objectionable outfits and prudish elders that possess some sort of administrative power exist, there will always be debate over what is appropriate to wear in public. And that topic is salacious enough to be worthy of a #1 hit. Try that on for size.

11

THE ARCHIES—"SUGAR, SUGAR" (1969)

t's January 1967. Don Kirshner, who procured the songs that would become hits for the Monkees, invited the four lads of the group to the Beverly Hills Hotel, where he had his own space rented for a media event that entailed presenting gold records and chunks of change to each member of the band. It was quite well known that the Monkees were a sham. All four members had to audition for the fictional band, whose records were promotional nuggets for the Screen Gems TV show of the same name. At the same time, these records—including the chart-toppers "Last Train to Clarksville" and "I'm a Believer"—became enormous hits. That's why Kirshner's job was crucial; he sourced the very songs from the likes of Neil Diamond, Carole King, and many others in order to provide for his phony band those gold records and hot checks.

Like plenty of other LA acts (as noted in the "This Diamond Ring" chapter), the Monkees were forced to use the Wrecking Crew for their musical services, only to add their vocals to the prerecorded tracks. As described in Kent Hartman's 2012 book *The Wrecking Crew: The Inside Story of Rock and Roll's Best-Kept Secret*, it was only a matter a time before frustration set in with members of the group, specifically the knit cap–topped Mike Nesmith, who was arguably the most serious musician and songwriter of the quartet. Back at the Beverly Hills Hotel, after the media scooted along from the press event, Kirshner presented the lads with some new songs he wanted them to record (or rather, the completed recordings he wanted to add their voices on to). This ticked off a perturbed Nesmith, who voiced his outrage at Kirshner for the group's lack of creative control and blurted out, "We're not recording for you anymore!" And things soon escalated when Kirshner's attorney, Herb Moelis, intervened with a read-your-contract response to Nesmith, who punched through the wall of the hotel before turning to Moelis and replying, "That could have been your face, motherfucker!"

Among the tunes Kirshner had presented to the band that fateful day was "Sugar, Sugar," a chintzy bubblegum rocker that sounded too cheesy even for the Monkees. However much of the ultrasweet song Nesmith and his gang had reviewed is unclear, but Nesmith's instincts seemed right when it came to rejecting the song (as ballsy as his protest was). So, two years later, Kirshner did the next best thing: He created a whole new fake group to record the song.

"Sugar, Sugar"—penned by producer-songwriter Jeff Barry and songwriter Andy Kim (who would later be responsible for the 1974 #1 hit "Rock Me Gently")—would be "performed" by a band emulating the characters from the *Archie* comics. Singers Ron Dante and Toni Wine sung the parts of the characters while session musicians (including Kim on guitar) handled the music. The gamble paid off, as "Sugar, Sugar" would soar to the #1 spot on the Hot 100 at the end of September 1969 and stick to the top like a gumdrop for four weeks.

Admittedly, "Sugar, Sugar" (another selection from the *Fun Rock* record set your body can't resist) has a highly infectious melody and snappy groove. The question is how could such an infantile tune hit the top of the charts the same year that Woodstock had wafted, the Manson Family slaughtered innocent people, and the Beatles, with hair spilling out of every hole in their heads, trotted across a street together for the very last time? As with "Honey," the song would have been a better fit years before its release. Even more mind-boggling is the fact that the chart-topping reign of "Sugar, Sugar" was sandwiched in between that of the Rolling Stones' "Honky Tonk Women" and the Temptations' "I Can't Get Next to You" (two songs that could easily kick Archie's ass and steal his lunch money). This was the summer of '69, a period Bryan Adams would later boast about for how cool the music and women were (even though he was only a child at the time). Why did America geek out for four weeks? The answer might have something to do with the Apollo 11 moon landing. No, really.

On July 20, 1969, while over a billion eyeballs were fixed on astronaut Neil Armstrong descending a ladder to destiny, Zager and Evans were scaring the hell out of everyone with "In the Year 2525," a tune that would dominate the top of the Hot 100 for six weeks. Following the historic lunar event, the upbeat (and undecipherable) "Honky Tonk Women" would take over the #1 spot for four weeks. Next up was "Sugar, Sugar." All these good vibes could very well have been a sign that America was seeking a more innocent time, right after so many people experienced an out-of-this-world milestone (and that will be the first and last dad joke to be told in this book). Still need more evidence? Look no further than "Someday We'll Be Together," an extraordinarily optimistic single by the Supremes, which would become the final Hot 100 chart-topper of the 1960s.

So, should "Sugar, Sugar"—the tune at the center of Mike Nesmith's January 1967 tirade—get a pass for its four-week run at the top and timelessness as an oldies fixture? In terms of its historical context, absolutely. But it still deserves to have a hole punched through it with a fist.

12

THREE DOG NIGHT—
"MAMA TOLD ME (NOT TO COME)" (1970)

At the dawn of the '70s, one of the hottest acts in the music business was Three Dog Night. And it's easy to see why. The pop-friendly septet was comprised of a tight rhythm section in support of three vocalists: Danny Hutton, Chuck Negron, and Cory Wells. These three singers couldn't have been more different from one another, yet when their voices blended, a three-part harmony would result that almost dared the Hot 100 to resist the group's pop prowess. Three Dog Night had the caliber of hits to walk the walk, scoring nearly a dozen Top 10 hits. Of those singles, three would manage to claim the top spot. And the most confounding of the trio, a cover of Randy Newman's "Mama Told Me (Not to Come)," happened to be the first.

Today, Randy Newman is a household name, thanks in no small part to Pixar. But in 1970, nobody really knew who he was as, up until that time, he was cranking out songs for the likes of the Fleetwoods and Dusty Springfield. "Mama Told Me (Not to Come)" was given by Newman to Eric Burdon and the Animals for their 1967 LP, *Eric Is Here*. The song, which describes a nervous geek dilly-dallying around a party that offers a cornucopia of illicit drugs, made enough of an impression on Cory Wells that he lobbied hard for Three Dog Night to record the song after the group completed their first two albums during the late '60s.

Wells's imploration must have been quite convincing. After releasing two consecutive Top 5 singles in 1969—Harry Nilsson's "One" and a cover of the *Hair* track "Easy to Be Hard"—Three Dog Night's momentum was starting to reverse. The band's take on Laura Nyro's "Eli's Coming" succeeded in barely making the Top 10, whereas the jubilant "Celebrate" stalled at #15. The group's next move would have to be a very careful one.

"Mama Told Me (Not to Come)" was becoming a distant memory (even for Animals fans), but Randy Newman would record a light-speed version of the song for his 1970 sophomore LP, *12 Songs*. In contrast to the Animals' 1967 version, which is built around a slow groove and emphasizes the "told" lyric on the first beat of the first measure of the chorus, Newman places the lyric on the first beat of the second measure, allowing for more space. Wells was evidently more favorable to the Animals' arrangement, as Three Dog Night would create a carbon copy of the music, using a Wurlitzer keyboard to mimic the reverb-soaked groove Eric Burdon and his band built for their original take.

And then Wells's vocal arrives.

Out of the slick rhythm pattern that emanates during the first four bars of the recording is a bizarre and jarring vocal that asks, "Won-som-whis-kee-in-yah-wah-tah-shoo-gah-wit-yo-tee?" When Cory sings these words—as if he were a pimp—the only reasonable explanation is that a gag vocal was mixed in by mistake. But no. Wells is *making fun* of Randy Newman's voice, phrasing the lyrics in a nasally, New Faux-leans vocal style. Like the Animals' recording, Three Dog Night's rendition puts the emphasis of the chorus hook on the first beat of the first measure, and in the place of Burdon's singular vocal is a remarkable three-part harmony by Hutton, Negron, and Wells. But Wells's ridiculous colloquial tongue at the verse sections—putting down the very composer who penned the song—is just too hard to get through. Nevertheless, the goofily sung single proceeded to top the Hot 100 for two weeks in July 1970.

Everybody loves a clown, but no one likes an asshole. However, Newman was not offended at all by the farce. As a matter of fact, he reportedly reached out to Wells and thanked him for putting his kids through college with his vocal satire. But Newman wasn't terribly impressed with the hit version and later commented in the 1998 box set *Guilty: 30 Years of Randy Newman*, "Three Dog Night changed it around so that the chorus would be more of a hook. [It] wouldn't [have] been a hit the way I did it, but I like it that way." Technically, Eric Burdon and the Animals first recorded "Mama Told Me (Not to Come)" the way Three Dog Night did but never had a hit from it. In essence, Three Dog Night was doing an impression of Randy Newman doing an impression of Eric Burdon. So, what's the deal?

It's quite possible listeners were so intrigued by the zany vocal that carries the Three Dog Night hit that even in the Google-less world that was 1970, many were curious enough to find out who this Randy Newman fellow was who wrote the tune. And once they heard Newman's brief *12 Songs* version of the track put out earlier that year, they decided Three Dog Night's version was better. Listeners liked silly. Listeners liked to move and groove. Listeners liked songs of debauchery. And, with all due respect to Mr. Newman, a group of dudes with tight pants and a little more sex appeal could better deliver it.

Three Dog Night's run of hits would continue, including two more chart-toppers: "Joy to the World" (1971) and "Black and White" (1972). As for Newman, both his bank account and notoriety would grow following Three Dog Night's chart success from "Mama Told Me (Not to Come)." The composer's 1971 *Live* LP would appropriately kick off with the very song that put his kids through college, and by the time Newman's critically acclaimed (and controversial) *Sail Away* album was issued in 1972, he was a household name, ranking with the likes of others in the singer-songwriter field like Cat Stevens and Carly Simon.

Cory Wells's envisagement of Three Dog Night recording an offbeat take on "Mama Told Me (Not to Come)" was a big risk that just happened to pay dividends. Music that borders on absurdity does in fact sell. If it didn't, we wouldn't still have Crash Test Dummies' "Mmm Mmm Mmm Mmm" moaning and croaking in our heads every once in a blue moon . . . you're thinking of it right now, aren't you?

13

DIANA ROSS—
"AIN'T NO MOUNTAIN HIGH ENOUGH" (1970)

When all is said and done, "Ain't No Mountain High Enough" will go down as one of the most memorable ditties within the Motown library. The tune has attained some major stamina throughout generations, whether it be the multitudes of cover versions that have been released over the past fifty years or countless scream-along performances that tend to bellow out on karaoke night. The song is a classic and really deserved a #1 placement on the Hot 100. Of course, this author is referring to the original 1967 recording by Marvin Gaye and Tammi Terrell as opposed to the weird, theatrical rendition put out by Diana Ross in 1970.

Nickolas Ashford and Valerie Simpson were perhaps the most successful songwriting duo in R&B history. Some of us '80s kids might recognize the married couple from their appearance in the MTV video in support of their 1984 single "Solid," which shows the twosome practically having a lip sync–induced orgasm underneath a bridge in Central Park. But Ashford and Simpson mastered the art of penning great duets, specifically for Motown stars Marvin Gaye and Tammi Terrell during the mid-1960s. Tunes like "Your Precious Love" and "Ain't Nothing Like the Real Thing" would edge into the Top 10 of both the R&B and Hot 100 charts, but 1967's "Ain't No Mountain High Enough" is what really put Ashford and Simpson—and the brief Gaye-Terrell hit catalog (Terrell would retire from the road in 1969 after being diagnosed with brain cancer, succumbing to the disease a year later)—on the map. The single would peak at the #19 spot on the Hot 100, climbing all the way to #3 on the R&B chart.

America was just getting a taste of the Gaye-Terrell singing team, which might explain the lukewarm peak placement of "Ain't No Mountain High Enough" within the Top 40. But the song had #1 hit written all over it. Diana Ross and the Temptations had at least an inkling of the song's potential and would include their own version on the teamed-up 1968 LP *Diana Ross & the Supremes Join the Temptations*. After leaving the Supremes in 1970, Ross would record her eponymous debut album, using the services of Ashford and Simpson to oversee the sessions and provide the material. "Reach Out and Touch (Somebody's Hand)" was the very single meant to launch Ross's solo career. Unfortunately, the tune would flatline at #20 on the Hot 100, leaving a very familiar song to save the day.

For the *Diana Ross* sessions, Ashford and Simpson would not only rework "Ain't No Mountain High Enough" but give it an absolute facelift for the album. The lyrics were rewritten, adding spoken-word sections for Ross to recite. With a lush orchestra backing the recording and a new introduction added, the song would clock in at over six minutes, with the chorus not kicking in until more than four minutes into the track. If it weren't for Ross vocalizing the melody of the chorus with (non-Supremes) backing singers, the tune would be 100 percent unrecognizable up until that four-minute mark. This is not Motown—it's Broadway. The emotional part of the track where Ross guarantees her wayward lover that he can always return to her could almost fit into the scene of *Grease 2* during which Stephanie bemoans her fallen motorcycle sweetheart at the high school talent show.

Oddly enough—with an edit of the track down to just over three minutes—"Ain't No Mountain High Enough" would be chosen to follow up the ill-fated "Reach Out and Touch (Somebody's Hand)" single. But disc jockeys would favor the unedited version of the track and play the full enchilada on the air. And wouldn't you know it? All six minutes of the single would scale the Hot 100 and grab the top spot in September 1970 for three weeks.

Diana Ross's take on "Ain't No Mountain High Enough" might have been unusual, but it was also an abnormality for what Motown was sending to the stores in 1970. The Jackson 5 was the hottest act on the label at the time, and the quintet would score a total of four #1 pop hits that year, including the exuberant ass-shakers "I Want You Back," "ABC," and "The Love You Save." 1970 would also produce the energetic Motown chart-toppers "War" (Edwin Starr) and "Tears of a Clown" (Smokey Robinson and the Miracles). How could a wordy, sorrowful time-sucker join the ranks of such hits?

The answer might have a lot to do with the fact that 1970 was a year that some exceptionally lugubrious ballads made their mark on the pop charts. Three of the year's biggest hits included the solemn "Bridge over Troubled Water" by Simon and Garfunkel (topping the Hot 100 for six weeks) and the final issued singles by the Beatles, "Let It Be" and "The Long and Winding Road." Both of those weepers would each claim the top spot for two weeks. "Ain't No Mountain High Enough" simply fit in with the pity party.

For Diana Ross, it probably didn't matter whether her version of "Ain't No Mountain High Enough" or the initial "Reach Out and Touch (Somebody's Hand)" single succeeded in grabbing the top spot. The singer proved she could be a solo force to be reckoned with. As for the remaining Supremes, they no longer had their former lead lady's name slapped at the front or back of their name. Meanwhile, Nickolas Ashford and Valerie Simpson picked up some extra royalty checks. So everybody wins.

On a related note, Ashford and Simpson would reunite with Diana Ross for the 1979 LP *The Boss*. The album's title track—an anthemic, disco heartbreaker—really, *really* should have topped the Hot 100, considering the polyester times during which it was released. Instead, the tune stalled at the #19 spot, failing to cut a rug with the best of them. In essence, "The Boss" suffered the curse of "Reach Out and Touch (Somebody's Hand)" but lacked an "Ain't No Mountain High Enough" to bail it out.

SLY AND THE FAMILY STONE—
"FAMILY AFFAIR" (1971)

As mentioned in the previous chapter, 1970 was the year where sad songs said so much. But Bay Area funk and soul ensemble Sly and the Family Stone certainly represented an exception with the phonetically titled "Thank You (Falettinme Be Mice Elf Agin)," which topped the Hot 100 for two weeks in February. The tune followed a string of hits by the group, including the boisterous 1967 single "Dance to the Music" (#8), 1969's "Hot Fun in the Summertime" (#2), and "Everyday People," which became their first chart-topper, hitting that mark for four straight weeks between February and March 1969.

But "Thank You" is pure magic. The hypnotizing track includes a smooth rhythm pattern by guitarist-keyboardist Sly (born Sylvester Stewart), brother Freddie on guitar, Larry Graham on bass, and Greg Errico rounding things out on drums. With support on trumpet and saxophone by Cynthia Robinson and Jerry Martini (respectively), Sly, sister Rose, and much of the band sing the praises of funk while name-dropping some of the band's previous singles. "Thank You" was a promise of fresh tunes for a fresh decade, put out by a mainstream group of a racially integrated makeup.

But then, disaster struck.

The same bubbly band that had been cranking out hit after hit at the end of the 1960s fell into a slump. At the dawn of the '70s, the Black Panther Party had approached Sly, demanding he kick out the two white members of the group. The front man wisely resisted, but the band had much bigger problems: hard drugs. Sly specifically dabbled in the activity of freebasing cocaine and was becoming increasingly difficult to work with in the studio and out on the road, where he was missing concert dates.

Epic Records (the group's label) had issued "I Want to Take You Higher" (previously the B-side to the band's 1969 "Stand!" single) as its own stand-alone single in March 1970, and it did edge into the Top 40, but by the fall of 1971, fans of Sly and the Family Stone were suffering from a major drought of listening material, as the band's shelf life was certainly starting to expire. During such a dynamic period in pop music history, any act that took more than a year to put out new music—especially if the material was about as far out as it can get from any commercial appeal—could pretty much count on that music going straight to the bargain bins. Once again, Sly and the Family Stone was the exception.

There's little doubt Epic was getting nervous about the arrival of the band's next long-player and would, throughout 1971, fittingly publicize their next album as *The Incredible and Unpredictable Sly & the Family Stone*. In November, the group would finally issue *There's a Riot Goin' On*, the title being an answer to Marvin Gaye's landmark 1971 LP, *What's Going On*. As for the content, it could very well have been recorded in an insane asylum. Still, many consider *There's a Riot Goin' On* a masterpiece worthy of articles, books, and special editions that would typically be devoted to a *Pet Sounds* or a *Dark Side of the Moon*. (Okay, maybe not *that* many editions.)

Whether *There's a Riot Goin' On* is a masterpiece or a disasterpiece, it's very hard to defend the album's leading single, "Family Affair." By the time of its recording, the band was so fractured that—aside from Sly and sister Rose—the only musicians present on the record were keyboardist Billy Preston and guitarist Bobby Womack. Noticeably absent was Errico, who was replaced by a cheap-sounding drum machine (a feature present on much of the *Riot* LP). But if the drum machine wasn't disconcerting enough, Sly's drug-induced voice could have peeled the paint right off the wall. Said Womack in Coral Amende's *Rock Confidential*, "He'd be lying on the piano whacked out of his brain when it was time to do a vocal, and they'd have to lay the microphone next to his head. That's why it came out, 'Waaan chiiiile grows up to beeee!' I had to laugh when I read about this new singing style of Sly's that was so raw. Man, he was just fucked up!" Womack wasn't exaggerating—Otis Campbell, the town drunk from *The Andy Griffith Show*, could have put down a better vocal than Sly. In fact, an engineer by the name of Richard Tilles was called in to severely remix the tracks to make the entire recording listenable. Yet "Family Affair"—in all its slurring wonder—ruled the Hot 100 for three weeks in December 1971.

It would be easy for yours truly to conclude that *Billboard* was suffering from yet another case of the wintertime blues (as it did almost a decade earlier with "Telstar") when "Family Affair" achieved a #1 placement on the Hot 100, but the answer could be less complicated than that.

It's obvious the public was hungry for more music by Sly and the Family Stone, but a year and a half is a very long time to wait; this is especially true during a time span in which the Beatles broke up, Jimi Hendrix and Janis Joplin died, and the Temptations went through at least three lineup changes. But it wouldn't be a long shot at all to say that Sly Stone was a little ahead of the game when he recorded "Family Affair." Sure, the singer might have consumed a lot of substances, but he was probably lucid enough to study what was happening on the charts.

Enter our old friend, "Mama Told Me (Not to Come)."

Whether Sly was a Three Dog Night fan or not, he was surely aware—at least subconsciously—of the freak success "Mama Told Me (Not to Come)" had achieved with such a silly lead vocal. And both that song and "Family Affair" aren't terribly different when it comes to the arrangement: kooky vocal performance at the verse sections, clear and precise vocal at the chorus sections.

Womack might have been right when describing Sly as "fucked up" during the "Family Affair" sessions, but there weren't too many other ways for the garbled-verse sections of the tune to be articulated. Sure, Sly sounds like a wino, but the vocal wouldn't have worked had the singer put the same oomph into it as he did on "Dance to the Music" or "Life." Sly gave the world a very strange piece of plastic that they couldn't stop listening to.

MICHAEL JACKSON—"BEN" (1972)

"Ben" is a thing of beauty. If there ever was a class that taught budding songwriters how to pen the perfect ballad, "Ben" would be in the syllabus. "Ben" has the distinct honor of being one of very few songs in which both the composition and performance fight each other all the way throughout the track to determine which has the upper hand. Yes, "Ben" should by no means be referred to as shit, but it should never have been a #1 hit.

As touched on earlier, the Jackson 5 left an indelible mark on the charts in 1970, notching a total of four chart-toppers on the Hot 100 by the end of that year. It was only a matter a time before the group's little charismatic leader, Michael, would start cranking out solo records of his own. Meanwhile, the Osmonds (Brigham Young's answer to the Jackson 5) were hot on their Motown counterpart's trail, snagging a #1 hit in the spring of 1971 with the goody-good pop staple "One Bad Apple." Like the Jackson 5, the Osmonds had their very own little star in Donny, who was only thirteen years old and ready for the *Tiger Beat* limelight after "One Bad Apple" had finished its five-week run at the top. Hence, the most banal crap was given to Osmond to lay down in the studio on his own, and he would manage to score a

#1 pop hit in September 1971 with "Go Away Little Girl." (Talk about a musical sphincter lock.)

"Go Away Little Girl" was first taken to the top of the Hot 100 by Steve Lawrence in 1963, and Osmond was just too stinking cute not to repeat this accomplishment. The recording was bubblegum pop to the utmost level. And the kids loved Donny, which translated into major dollar signs. (Remember, brats listen to records, too.)

The kids also loved Michael Jackson, who had just turned thirteen before the release of his October 1971 debut single, "Got to Be There," which would barely edge into the Top 5. It wasn't a bad showing, although listeners might have been a little disturbed by a child singing about waking up in the morning with a lover. (Hold your jokes!) Jackson would next record a cover of Bobby Day's "Rockin' Robin" in February 1972. It was cheesy, lame, and nauseating. It was perfect. But somehow, the single stopped in its tracks after achieving a #2 placement on the Hot 100. Jackson's tepid follow-up 1972 singles, "I Wanna Be Where You Are" (stalling at #16) and a cover of Bill Withers's "Ain't No Sunshine" (not charting at all), made it seem as though the adolescent's star was falling before it could reach the top. But that notion was soon quelled, thanks to a psychopathic rodent.

In 1971, a low-budget flick called *Willard*—centered around a disgruntled man utilizing his rats to murder people— would gather enough box office receipts to warrant a 1972 sequel, *Ben*. In *Ben*, the titular rat would bypass any human orders and take his vermin buddies on an indiscriminate killing spree. With this sequel came the ballad "Ben," a sweet tune written by Don Black and Walter Scharf that served as an ode to the bond between a young boy and the very killer rat that wreaks havoc in the film. The spine-tingling orchestral arrangement adds a trepidation that could only mean the furry killer was coming to chew your face right off. What's really unsettling about "Ben" is the fact that the song plays at the end of the film while the credits roll. It would be as if "That's What Friends Are For" was chosen to play during the end titles of *A Nightmare on Elm Street*.

Whether or not Black and Scharf even watched *Willard* to understand what it would really be like to have a friend like Ben, Donny Osmond was the first candidate considered to belt out the song. It only made sense for a youngster who had melted young hearts at grade schools everywhere in 1971 with "Go Away Little Girl," as well as an extra-sugary take on Paul Anka's "Puppy Love" (which landed in the Top 5 earlier in 1972), to tackle the ballad. But Michael Jackson would ultimately be chosen to record "Ben." It was a wise decision.

With no shortage of controversies surrounding Jackson during much of his adult life (to be as diplomatic as possible), it's easy to forget how much of a consummate entertainer the artist was as a youth. Barely fourteen years old, the singer's phrasing of "Ben" is absolutely stunning. And, despite the song's flesh-eating subject, it's a beautifully written ballad.

But what exactly compelled "Ben" to top the Hot 100 in October 1972 (let alone be nominated for an Academy Award the following year)? The *Willard* "franchise" wasn't exactly intended for a younger viewing audience. Even if it were, kids certainly wouldn't have wind-sprinted out of the theaters after the movie was over to beg their mothers to buy them the "Ben" single. Trust me, I remember Michael Jackson's popularity very well during the early '80s; the kids wanted to hear "Billie Jean," not "The Girl Is Mine."

The explanation behind the success of "Ben" might have to do with the fact that Jackson had a major growth spurt as an artist during the year 1972. Whereas "Rockin' Robin" was marketed toward a younger listener, God knows who "Ben" was intended for. But adults were obviously beginning to take the singer seriously, as Jackson had belted out one doozie of a tearjerker that was certainly not meant as a stocking stuffer for children.

After enjoying a #1 hit, Michael Jackson would refocus his efforts on his work with his brothers during the rest of the '70s and would have to wait seven years before his landmark *Off the Wall* album would provide him with his next #1 hit, "Don't Stop 'Til You Get Enough." And the rest, as you know, is HIStory. Jackson's subsequent run of hits—and questionable lifestyle—would leave his beautiful reading of "Ben" so far back in the dust, many are surprised to find out the song was in fact the artist's first chart-topper—yet not nearly as surprised to learn the song is about a rat. And a murderous one at that.

CHUCK BERRY—"MY DING-A-LING" (1972)

R ight after "Ben" had finished its week-long run at the top of the Hot 100 in October 1972, the chart supposedly suffered a head injury. That must be the only explanation as to why a turd of a song called "My Ding-a-Ling" took over the top spot for two full weeks. And, pathetically, it was done courtesy of one of rock and roll music's most adored legends.

Before his 2017 death, Chuck Berry likely did not want his epitaph to mention anything about his sole chart-topper (as much as he would have not wanted it to mention his sordid past with the law [again, to be diplomatic]). The cocky guitar god's legacy was sealed during the 1950s by means of timeless rock standards like "Johnny B. Goode" and "Rock and Roll Music" and further carried on via countless covers by rock acts such as the Beatles, the Rolling Stones, and the Beach Boys (who would surprisingly score a Top 10 hit in 1976 with the latter tune). Berry—a singer, songwriter, and masterful performer—came as a whole package. But by the early '70s, the artist was nothing more than a limp relic from a long gone era. So when Berry was invited to participate in the February 1972 Lancaster Arts Festival in London (preceding Pink Floyd, for crying out loud), he whipped out something quite memorable, yet highly disturbing.

Amid a set list that included just a hint of Chuck Berry standards like "Johnny B. Goode" and "Sweet Little Sixteen" was a tune of extraordinary length. It was Berry's eleven-plus-minute rendition of a 1952 novelty record by David Bartholomew called "My Ding-a-Ling," a sassy ode to . . . well, you've probably figured it out by now. On it, Berry leads the very-British audience on a sing-along of the chorus while he shoves in the double entendre–loaded verse sections, all the while accompanying himself with some steady rhythm work on his axe. The song is total junk, but everyone in the crowd seems to be having a good time (although it could be that they were just too high *not* to have a good time).

Berry had never enjoyed a #1 hit with his past rockers, but lightning seemed to strike the rod with "My Ding-a-Ling." Seven minutes were lopped off the performance (which could be heard in its entirety on the artist's hybrid studio/live *The London Chuck Berry Sessions* LP) for a four-minute single, which took over the #1 position on the Hot 100 during the final two weeks of October 1972.

Did "My Ding-a-Ling" benefit from a lack of good material on the charts, or was the tune just too naughty for people not to pick up the seven-inch pleaser at the record store? My bet is on the latter. On the track, Berry teases the audience as being "future Parliament," while some of the jokes he makes at the expense of certain members of the crowd are a little hard to decipher. It's certainly not the typical single designed to arouse the American consumer. Still, obscene music can be quite popular, and if nothing else, customers could have picked up a copy of the single and discreetly brought their lowbrow friends over to giggle around their well-endowed stereo system while the record was playing.

The timing surrounding the rise of "My Ding-a-Ling" was interesting in that the song's two-week run at the #1 position occurred just before the presidential election of 1972. Were younger listeners a little naive about George McGovern's chances against then-President Richard Nixon and started celebrating prematurely with such an idiotic tune? Were younger people just plain delirious after giving up on McGovern's odds and accepted Nixon's inevitable second term? While either scenario might be a stretch, Johnny Nash's sweet and carefree "I Can See Clearly Now" (which many consider to be the first reggae chart-topper) would find itself atop the Hot 100 for the entire month of November. Could it be that listeners wanted something bright, sunny, and less phallic to help them get their kicks?

There surely is a point to be made that listeners' attraction to "My Ding-a-Ling" was simply a short-term adolescent phase and they were ready to move on to something a little more dignified like the Nash tune. While "I Can See Clearly Now" was ruling the airways, the fleeting weeks of 1972 indeed seemed to be signaling peace and tranquility in America. But the goodwill wouldn't last very long. Warm and fuzzy turned into serious and topical on the Hot 100 during the month of December, with the Temptations' "Papa Was a Rollin' Stone" (deadbeat daddies), Helen Reddy's "I Am Woman" (feminism), and Billy Paul's "Me and Mrs. Jones" (adultery) taking turns claiming the top spot. But at least everyone, for the most part, kept it in their pants.

then-President Richard Nixon and started questioning

THE ROLLING STONES—"ANGIE" (1973)

There's no doubt the Rolling Stones are easily rock music's most enduring act. The group was started by multi-instrumentalist Brian Jones during the early '60s, but the creative force behind the Stones had always been the mouthful of a front man known as Mick Jagger and his indestructible counterpart, Keith Richards. Much ado has been made of the narcotics Richards has taken over the years, but both Jagger and Richards had consumed enough chemicals during the '60s and '70s to have killed more wild horses than the ones that attempted to drag Jagger away. Of course, the duo were Boy Scouts in comparison to the chemically induced Jones, who was dismissed from the very group he had founded (just before being found dead in his swimming pool in July 1969).

Still, through all the purple haze, Jagger and Richards had penned some unforgettable rockers and managed to land for the group five US chart-toppers before the close of the '60s. Even after their brethren from Liverpool had hung it all up in 1970, the Rolling Stones chugged right along and scored their sixth #1 single with "Brown Sugar" from their lauded 1971 *Sticky Fingers* LP. The Stones could do no wrong at the start of a new decade.

But the narcotics—as well as a reasonable tax gripe—would soon make things a little tricky for the group.

To avoid a steep tax rate from recording in their native England, the Stones decided to relocate to France and record many of the tracks for their 1972 double-LP, *Exile on Main St.*, there. The album would bear one decent hit for the group, "Tumbling Dice." It's a tune that might be a little on the incoherent side yet would still break the Top 10. But the French venture would be limited to just the one LP release, as Richards, along with then-lover Anita Pallenberg, would soon be facing a serious bust for heroin possession. The Stones had to, once again, find a new recording locale for their follow-up disc, and it seemed that only one country in the world would take them in.

With sessions beginning in October 1972, the band would make Kingston, Jamaica, their home and park it at Dynamic Sound Studios to record the tracks for what would become *Goats Head Soup*. Reggae masters Bob Marley and Jimmy Cliff had both previously recorded at Dynamic Sound, so the studio supposedly had some magic to it (as well as plenty of cannabis remnants). Elton John would inauspiciously attempt to record *Goodbye Yellow Brick Road* at Dynamic Sound later in 1973 before departing in horror due to the studio conditions, but the Stones apparently had no major technical issues during their stay. In fact, the Dynamic Sound sessions proved to be quite productive. Unfortunately, the material sucked.

"Doo Doo Doo Doo Doo (Heartbreaker)" had some hit potential (despite needing some of the doo-doo removed from the title). But, if only by default, "Angie" would become the standout track from *Goats Head Soup*. The sullen, minor-key ballad was composed mostly by Richards, and lots of speculation has since swirled as to who inspired the toxic rocker to compose the tune. The potential subject has included everyone from his daughter Dandelion to David Bowie's then-wife Angela.

But Jagger is the one who really sells "Angie" with his nearly comical "AYYN-JAY" vocal phrasing. The mood of the song is highly reminiscent of the Stones' 1971 ballad "Wild Horses," which just edged into the Top 30. So when "Angie" was issued as the first single from *Goats Head Soup*, it should've achieved a similar milestone. Instead, it freakishly topped the Hot 100 for one week in October 1973.

The chart-topping success of "Angie" might have caused many to believe they were living in a world of make-believe. And they might have been right. First off, the song was mixed quite poorly. If you listen closely to Jagger's vocal, there's a faint but audible noise that's either the lead singer's original guide vocal or the moaning and groaning of someone in the studio who had just downed ten bottles of Red Stripe. But bad mixing never hindered the success of previous Rolling Stones singles. On the group's 1967 hit "Let's Spend the Night Together," several random and uneven clicks can be heard, which is the sound of Jagger beating together nightsticks that belonged to two cops who dropped by the late-night recording session. (Producer Andrew Loog Oldham offered to make the officers' equipment famous to distract them from all the drugs lying around in the studio.)

Secondly, despite a gorgeous string arrangement by Nicky Harrison and Nicky Hopkins's suave piano playing, the song kind of just repeats itself and doesn't go much further than the addition of a bridge section that mixes up the chord progression. But keep in mind the Stones' first US #1 hit, "(I Can't Get No) Satisfaction," is not exactly a suite in seven parts.

Less could very well have been more when it came to "Angie." Some listeners will fight you to the death on how much a classic-rock juggernaut the Stones' 1972 *Exile on Main St.* is, whereas others might prefer to use the thick two-record set to prop up the broken leg of a dinner table. But the undeniable fact is *Exile on Main St.* has a whole lot of output on all four sides of it. Listeners wanted something simpler and, although *Goats Head Soup* is by no means an essential album, it indeed fits the mold of what the occasional Rolling Stones fans wanted: ten songs with a hit or two in the track listing. Fortunately for "Angie," it just happened to be the lucky winner.

RINGO STARR—"YOU'RE SIXTEEN" (1974)

It might surprise many to know that former Beatles drummer Ringo Starr holds the distinguished honor of having the most successful album in the US, at least by means of containing two chart-toppers. The aptly titled *Ringo* LP, released in 1973, is somewhat of a Beatles reunion. All three of the drummer's former bandmates drop by at some point during the album to supply compositions and studio help. John Lennon's contribution is the hubristic "I'm the Greatest," while Paul McCartney brings along the throwaway ballad "Six O'Clock."

But George Harrison proved to be the most productive ex-Beatle during the *Ringo* sessions, co-writing "Photograph" with Starr and adding some background vocals. The tune is pure beauty, featuring a robust string arrangement by Phil Spector's Wall of Sound maestro Jack Nitzsche. "Photograph" was the first single to be released from *Ringo* and would deservedly top the Hot 100 in November of 1973. Had Ringo recorded "Tie a Yellow Ribbon Round the Ole Oak Tree" (as originally intended) earlier that year, "Photograph" could easily have been his second #1 hit. But the former mop top would have to wait only two short months for his second US chart-topper. And it came in the form of a bizarre choice of a cover tune.

Aside from "Photograph," *Ringo* has its fair share of potential hits like the Harrison-penned "Sunshine Life for Me (Sail Away Raymond)" and the Starr–Vini Poncia collaboration "Oh My My" (which would become a Top 10 hit later in 1974). Even a cover of "Have You Seen My Baby"—by the now go-to songwriter Randy Newman—had merit.

But Ringo's buoyant take on the 1960 Johnny Burnette hit, "You're Sixteen," would get the green light. The song was written by brothers Richard and Robert Sherman—who would later go on Disney's payroll and compose the tunes for *Mary Poppins*, *The Jungle Book*, and many other films—and serves as an ode to a high school sweetheart courtesy of either her same-aged boyfriend or someone who really needs to register as a sex offender. (For the sake of argument, let's assume it's the former.) Burnette's fiery 1960 rendition, augmented with a brisk string arrangement, is the stuff made for malt shops where class rings and letterman jackets are passed between acne-laden lovers. Starr's version, however, brings things to a steady shuffle with the artist pounding away on a trap kit, alongside fellow drummer Jim Keltner. The itinerant Nicky Hopkins—fresh off his *Goats Head Soup* stint with the Rolling Stones—adds a pounding piano accompaniment, while Starr's drinking buddy, Harry Nilsson, overdubs some Schmilsson-esque harmonies. All the while, Paul McCartney takes care of the solo section by making kazoo noises through his cupped hand. It's a novelty record—right?

Starr's cover of "You're Sixteen" could be taken either as a novelty record or merely a Ringo-just-being-Ringo record. And the powers that be indeed put their bets on something a little more lighthearted for a follow-up single to the solemn and anthemic "Photograph," with the apparent gamble being that listeners would be rocking and rolling to a song containing a fake kazoo solo. However, there might have been a method to this madness, as just a couple of weeks before "You're Sixteen" reached the top of the Hot 100 in January 1974, Steve Miller's "The Joker" (you know, the song with the tongue-rolling "Mooooorrrrrrice" in the lyrics and cat-call whistles produced by a slide guitar) had briefly occupied the spot.

But unlike "The Joker," "You're Sixteen" was a product of a golden era immortalized by the highly successful 1973 George Lucas film *American Graffiti* and its accompanying soundtrack (which included Burnette's original 1960 release of the song). Sock hop classics were all the rage again, as evidenced by the Beach Boys' chart-topping and multiplatinum success the following year via the two-LP set *Endless Summer*, filled with all the band's '60s-era hits. *American Graffiti* was a watershed moment for oodles of shitty covers to come, and Starr might simply have been riding a wave of nostalgia that carried the ex-Beatle all the way to the top. If I were a betting man, I would wager on this explanation.

But whatever the case might have been, "You're Sixteen" would allow Starr to join both Paul McCartney and George Harrison in the club of solo Beatles with two US #1 hits under their belts. (John Lennon would have to wait until late 1974 for his collaboration with Elton John, "Whatever Gets You thru the Night," to hit the top. More on this in a few.)

The Ringo-just-being-Ringo theory, however, might have some legitimacy to it. If Starr had recorded the aforementioned "Tie a Yellow Ribbon Round the Ole Oak Tree" or, hell, even "My Ding-a-Ling," they would easily have been well loved. People are interested in Ringo—after all, the drummer did receive the most fan mail during the Beatles' heyday. Still, the oldies revival certainly had an impact on Starr and all involved in the promotion of his records. The proof of this is in the fact that the drummer would, in 1974, release an acoustic guitar-drenched version of the Platters' "Only You (And You Alone)" and still score a #6 placement on the Hot 100. Starr knew exactly how to turn the moldy oldies into goldies.

BLUE SWEDE—
"HOOKED ON A FEELING" (1974)

What the hell is an ooga-chaka?

There are more than enough imbecilic tunes out there that lead us to question the dexterity of their run on the Hot 100 (including a few examples previously mentioned in this book) or even the respectability of the Hot 100 itself. What makes the 1974 chart-topping status of Blue Swede's take on "Hooked on a Feeling" especially bewildering is the fact that the track is a cover *of* a cover of a song that probably should've been left alone in the first place.

Backing up a few years, late crooner B. J. Thomas would score his first big hit with 1969's "Hooked on a Feeling," which was written by Mark James (who was also responsible for Elvis Presley's "Suspicious Minds" and Thomas's previous Top 40 single, "The Eyes of a New York Woman"). "Hooked on a Feeling" would earn for Thomas a #5 showing on the Hot 100 and kick off a subsequent string of hits for the singer, including the 1970 chart-topper "Raindrops Keep Falling on My Head." Thomas's original recording of "Hooked on a Feeling" is one funky mo-fo.

Beginning with a melody played by an electric sitar (which was out of vogue by a couple years), Thomas bellows out the lyrics, as supported by an overly excited string ensemble. The song has such a feel-good vibe, it's impossible not to adore it.

Fast-forward to 1971. British singer-songwriter Jonathan King would resurrect "Hooked on a Feeling," adding a faux-reggae beat and some backing voices that sound like a perpetual "ooga-ooga" hiccup. This effect was supposedly inspired by the same noises heard on a shithole of a chart-topper by Johnny Preston from 1959 called "Running Bear." King's rendition of "Hooked on a Feeling" wouldn't do jack squat on the US charts but would crack the Top 40 in the artist's native England.

Two years later, a Swedish rock act by the hardy-har-har moniker of Blue Swede would ape King's version of "Hooked on a Feeling"—adding full-throated "ooga-chakas" to their recording, cleaning up some of the drug-related puns in the lyrics, and amplifying the horn arrangement to the decibel level of a mariachi band—for a 1973-issued single. By April of the following year, it would wander all the way up to the top spot of the Hot 100. Somewhere, a young David Hasselhoff must have made a vow he would record a campy version of "Hooked on a Feeling" that would show up the Blue Swede version. He would do so over two decades later and, frankly, it wasn't much worse.

How exactly a small-beans band from Sweden rose to the top with a tune that was already done before (twice) is a head-scratcher, but we can certainly rule out the group's shared nationality with ABBA. The latter Swedish hit-making quartet was still a year or so away from making a major impression on the US charts and had barely put out their breakthrough Top 10 single, "Waterloo." America fell in love with Blue Swede and its abrasive single for God knows why. Yet God might have been onto something.

Blue Swede's corny version of "Hooked on a Feeling" could have benefited from a word-of-mouth buzz, long before social media was invented. Apparently, a record store owner in Connecticut played the imported disc in the store over and over, which led to local radio stations rotating it until the tune spread across the country like the plague. The same thing happened with Elton John's "Bennie and the Jets," which was never intended to be a single. But as a result of constant radio airplay at a Detroit-area station and some finagling on the part of Elton's US marketing team, "Bennie and the Jets" would end up at the top of the Hot 100 in 1974 (interestingly, the week following "Hooked on a Feeling's" one-week run).

But unlike the original quirky track that is "Bennie and the Jets," "Hooked on a Feeling" is a cover—and an obnoxious one. Besides, it's a little hard to believe that the grassroots effort behind the Blue Swede single alone catapulted it into pop stardom. Much like a Tickle Me Elmo doll or *Seinfeld*, annoying crap will always find a home in pop culture. And "Hooked on a Feeling" was no exception. Decades after the tune reared its ugly face on the charts, it would appear in several films and TV sitcoms like *Reservoir Dogs*, *Guardians of the Galaxy*, and *3rd Rock from the Sun*. So it's hard to argue against the impression the track has since made on generations of listeners.

It's also important to note that right around the time "Hooked on a Feeling" bubbled to the top of the Hot 100, Robert Opel famously streaked across the stage at the 46th Academy Awards ceremony, setting the stage for Ray Stevens's "The Streak" to snag a three-week chart-topping run beginning in May. (We can now conclude how *that* shit became a #1 hit.) Obviously, there was a lot of laughing gas in the air that would allow for "Hooked on a Feeling" to claim the top spot. Regardless, the song is total garbage, and far more than enough has now been written about it in this chapter.

20

PAUL ANKA— "(YOU'RE) HAVING MY BABY" (1974)

August 24, 1974. It was a dark day in the history of the *Billboard* Hot 100. It's the date that would mark the first of a three-week stretch of the chart-topping run of a single that could only be described as stomach-turning . . . or, more appropriately, womb-turning.

Paul Anka had a pen in countless hits spanning the '60s and '70s, whether it be his 1960 saccharine teenybopper anthem "Puppy Love" or Tom Jones's 1971 ball-busting rocker, "She's a Lady." But Anka's lyrical contribution to the 1969 Frank Sinatra standard "My Way"—and, not to mention, his penning of "Johnny's Theme" for *The Tonight Show*—truly solidified his place in the Songwriters Hall of Fame, as well as earning for him kudos in his native Ottawa in the form of a plenitude of awards and street names.

But the apex of Anka's commercial highlights involves a tune orated through the perspective of a soon-to-be father who sounds almost as if he's holding his pregnant partner hostage in a cellar. Yes, it's the infamous ode to spreading one's seed—"(You're) Having My Baby." Just the odd placement of the parentheses is a little creepy. But once the easygoing '70s-style winds kick off the introduction, we're in for a long ride through Disturbland. Anka starts off the vocals, gushing over what is going and growing inside his baby mama. Then, in what represents at least a tiny bit of relief, a female voice—that of singer Odia Coates—concurs with Anka about what is going and growing inside of her. But when Anka suggests his baby-bumped gal could have "swept" it from her life, the only thing you want to abort is the song. (Did I happen to mention this is the same guy who cowrote "My Way"?)

"(You're) Having My Baby" would become Anka's first #1 hit on the Hot 100 since his 1959 single, "Lonely Boy," reached the top while the singer was at the ripe old age of seventeen. Despite the songwriting credits Anka had racked up in the fifteen years since his last chart-topper, why in the world would a song that makes "Honey" sound like "Iron Man" serve as the comeback hit that would put the artist back on top?

Let's first look at the social implications of "(You're) Having My Baby." (God, I hate those parentheses.) The 1973 *Roe v. Wade* decision was still relatively fresh in the minds of Americans. So when Anka concedes that his lady had every right to terminate the pregnancy, yet celebrates her decision to keep the baby, both sides of the hot-button issue could easily have claimed victory. Then again, Anka made a few enemies with the song. The National Organization for Women slapped him with a "Keep Her in Her Place" award for portraying the female subject in the song as an obsequious dolt. The "Puppy Love" singer was suddenly a controversial figure.

What about the music itself? The breezy nature of the accompaniment—bringing to mind images of wood panels and avocado-colored appliances—could perfectly fit inside the confines of an elevator. But remember that this was 1974, the same year that softies like "Love's Theme" and "The Way We Were" were battling one another for the top spot.

As far as the political component of "(You're) Having My Baby," it's tough to believe the tune served as a rallying cry either for or against abortion. As icky as the "swept" lyric might be, it pales in comparison to much of the rest of the ickiness heard throughout the song. And although it might have served as a handy paperweight, the "Keep Her in Her Place" award had little effect on the chart action of Anka's song.

In essence, "(You're) Having My Baby" was a freeway accident that was just too hard to turn away from, and listeners, much like bloodthirsty motorists, gave it their undivided attention. The same could be said of later *Billboard* hits that drew equal gag reflexes as they did successful chart activity, including mid-1990s hits "Cotton Eye Joe" (Rednex) and "Tootsee Roll" (69 Boyz). But while both of those tunes made impressive showings on the Hot 100, neither reached the top of the chart, thus bringing up the question of what made the Anka tune so special for it to do so. Hey, it was the batshit-crazy '70s.

STEVIE WONDER—
"YOU HAVEN'T DONE NOTHIN'" (1974)

Stevie Wonder was on a roll by 1974. Since the start of the decade, the Motown great was putting out material with full creative control. This began in 1971 with the LP *Where I'm Coming From*, which led to the 1972 classics *Music of My Mind* and *Talking Book*, the latter of which spawned the two chart-toppers "Superstition" and "You Are the Sunshine of My Life." 1973's *Innervisions*—one of the greatest albums of all time, period—would further expand the musical landscape of Wonder's noggin via the Top 10 social-commentary singles "Higher Ground" (later covered by the Red Hot Chili Peppers) and "Living For the City." Wonder's early '70s output was legendary, owing much of its success to TONTO (The Original New Timbral Orchestra), an electronic interface developed by New York-based music tech wizards Malcom Cecil and Robert Margouleff.

Following the success of *Innervisions*—and after surviving a serious car accident that put the artist in a coma for a week— Wonder was back in action in 1974 to do more damage to the

Hot 100 via his Top 5 gift to Rufus, "Tell Me Something Good." That summer, he would issue the horribly titled *Fulfillingness' First Finale* (believe it or not, there was to be a *Fulfillingness' Second Finale* before the idea was nixed for his 1976 multidisc masterpiece, *Songs in the Key of Life*), featuring "Boogie on Reggae Woman." It's a track with a super funky groove, yet an almost-muddled vocal and closing harmonica solo that goes on for days, making it seem as though the track was unfinished. Despite all its blemishes, "Boogie on Reggae Woman" would shoot all the way up to the #3 spot on the Hot 100, following its late-1974 single release. But the success of its preceding single is the real wonder.

Without a doubt, the plight of President Richard Nixon, facing an inevitable impeachment resulting from the investigation into the Watergate scandal, was the biggest story of 1974. And just before Nixon's resignation in August of that year, Stevie Wonder would issue a diatribe against Tricky Dick in the form of "You Haven't Done Nothin'." By November, the single would become a #1 pop hit. The clavinet-driven track—caked with a fierce horn section and some backup vocals by the Jackson 5— certainly has a lot of energy to it, as evident in Wonder's accusatory lyrics that make it clear as to the artist's feelings toward the thirty-seventh president of the United States.

But the tune has its share of problems. Firstly, the song title—which suggests Wonder considers Nixon derelict of his duties—might imply, ironically, that the troubled leader of the free world "hasn't done nothin' wrong" in the scope of his legal woes. More appropriately, the song should have been titled "You're in Deep Shit." Secondly, the Jackson 5's contribution to the track involves a series of half-assed "doo-doo-wops" at the break sections. Sure, it's a Stevie Wonder record, but using one of the hottest groups in the business to provide such a minor role on the record is like calling Willie Mays up to the plate to carry out a sacrifice bunt.

The third issue with "You Haven't Done Nothin'" might provide some insight as to how the song made it to the top of the Hot 100 (and *three* whole months after Nixon made his famous peace signs in front of 1600 Pennsylvania Avenue). Even for the occasional Stevie Wonder listener, it's impossible not to notice the similarities between "You Haven't Done Nothin'" and 1972's "Superstition." Whether or not Wonder had intended this cloning, Motown's collective mouth was surely watering over it. The label had mastered the art of putting out doppelgänger singles by several of their artists (see the early works of the Supremes and the Four Tops). So would it really be such a bad thing to release "Superstition Part 2"? Nope—and Motown would log yet another chart-topper in the pop world.

But when it comes to celebrating the most successful output of Stevie Wonder, "You Haven't Done Nothin'" rarely comes up in the same breath as "You Are the Sunshine of My Life," "I Just Called to Say I Love You," or—yes—"Superstition." It's just not memorable. And while today's news cycle is a hell of a lot faster than it was back in the '70s, three months since the political figure in question had resigned from office is a very long time-lapse for anyone to give a rat's ass as to how well he was doing at his job before he quit.

Putting aside the similarity with "Superstition," could there be a technical reason as to why "You Haven't Done Nothin'" became a #1 hit in November 1974? If I were a conspiracy theorist, I could suggest radio listeners and record store customers alike could have confused the nomenclature of the song with Bachman-Turner Overdrive's very own double-negative anthem, "You Ain't Seen Nothing Yet," which claimed the top spot right after Wonder's song had finished its weeklong run. But then I would sound like one of those nuts who attributed the #1 status of Lorne Greene's "Ringo" to a mix-up with a member of the Beatles. Or would I?

22

BILLY SWAN—"I CAN HELP" (1974)

If you're as old as me, you more than likely, as a kid, made plenty of trips to gimmicky pizza parlors with your friends for birthday parties. It would be at these child-centric locales where you'd bring the Transformer your mom had bought and wrapped for you as a gift for the snot-nosed birthday boy and proceed to spend most of your time in the arcade room with a stack of quarters.

For those of you '80s kids who were very lucky, you might remember going to a local ShowBiz Pizza Place where—along with the usual arcade games and gizmos—there was an in-house band of giant animatronic characters called the Rock-afire Explosion. These behemoths were programmed to simulate movements on their instruments while lip-syncing to incredibly corny music that was prerecorded. The show wasn't exactly the coolest thing for a kid to experience, but it was at least something to watch while eating slices of cardboard topped with ketchup and pepperoni. Billy Swan's "I Can Help," which topped the Hot 100 for the final two weeks in November 1974, could have easily fit into the Rock-afire Explosion's set list.

The Missouri-born Swan would, by the 1960s, become quite the utility man in Nashville, whether it be musician, songwriter, roadie, or studio custodian. He would find steady work as the bassist in Kris Kristofferson's touring band in 1970 and eventually snag a recording deal with Monument Records. Aside from the experience of playing live music on the road with an established artist, the most advantageous thing about Swan's affiliation with Kristofferson would involve a cheap-sounding RMI organ the latter and his then-wife Rita Coolidge would bestow upon him as a birthday gift (presumably not at a pizza parlor). It would be on this instrument that Swan would compose the rockabilly-styled "I Can Help," a tune that finds the narrator—with two strong arms, mind you—pleading to a love interest to take him up on his offer to be her main squeeze, even offering to be a stepfather to her children. Yikes.

Potential restraining orders aside, the recording itself probably should have had a few more bucks thrown at it. While Swan left his RMI at home for the sessions, an equally bad Farfisa organ would be utilized by the artist for the actual recording. It was a portable version of the Farfisa, as provided by keyboardist Bobby Emmons (he did help). Kicking off with a Chuck Berry–like guitar intro, the organ comes in and resonates like a migraine. It's almost as if the organist from a pizza and pipes joint stopped by to show everyone what pain and suffering truly is. After Swan is finished with his groveling, the tune winds down to a droning organ chord before revving right back up amid a curious sound of applause. The same stop-and-go trick repeats before the track fades out of its misery.

I'm not going to lie: "I Can Help" is a cute little ditty that fits right in with the oddball ethos of the mid-1970s. But topping the Hot 100 for two consecutive weeks? (At least we knew listeners were well over Richard Nixon by then.) *Billboard* was certainly in a whimsical mood in November 1974. Before "I Can Help" made its mark at the top of the Hot 100, it was preceded by the jovial "Whatever Gets You thru the Night," John Lennon's first #1 hit—and the only chart-topper the former Beatle would enjoy while still living—which he had recorded with Elton John. (In fact, while "I Can Help" was dominating the pop world, Lennon would, after losing a bet with Elton that "Whatever Gets You thru the Night" wouldn't reach the top, perform with the bespectacled piano star at Madison Square Garden in New York City on Thanksgiving Day.)

So that must be it: America was so mellowed-out by the end of 1974 and only needed happy hits to get by. (This certainly explains why Carl Douglas's ridiculous "Kung Fu Fighting" would follow "I Can Help" with a two-week run of its own at the top.) One thing for sure is that Billy Swan sounds like he's having a ball on his lone chart-topper, much like those animatronic characters appeared while they were getting down in the Rock-afire Explosion band. Their smiles are surely still frozen on their dust-gathering bodies in a warehouse somewhere in the Midwest, where one or two cheap, antiquated organs are probably stored as well.

THE CARPENTERS—
"PLEASE MR. POSTMAN" (1975)

It's hard to believe crack cocaine wasn't around in 1975 since, considering what was popular in music at the time, people seemed to be smoking quite a lot of it. At the beginning of the year, "Kung Fu Fighting" was still stinking up the charts in its sweaty *gi*, while Sammy Johns was trying to lure everybody into his Chevy van. As Paul Anka and Odia Coates were still celebrating the act of baby-making, many were hoping an axe murderer would meet Donny and Marie on their morning side of the mountain. The Bee Gees, meanwhile, decided to give everyone a crash course on what they thought the meaning of "jive" was. And you know things were bad when even Alice Cooper was getting soft on us.

Indeed, 1975 offered a treasure trove of crap when it came to pop music (and we haven't even touched on Captain & Tennille). There is just too much shit to mention. But to stay true to the idea of this book to separate the über-successfully crappy from the merely crappy—and considering that we need to move on at some point—I narrowed down the worst of the

1975 chart-toppers to six songs. And the Carpenters have the unfortunate honor of being the first casualty.

The toothy brother and sister duo from Connecticut celebrated a stack of hits during the first half of the '70s. But as vanilla as Karen and Richard Carpenter's act was during this era, the inimitable vocal style of the former made it understandable as to how the two scored ten Top 10 hits from 1970 to 1973, including the chart-toppers "(They Long to Be) Close to You" (a Burt Bacharach–Hal David composition originally cut by Richard Chamberlain in 1963) and "Top of the World." The Carpenters got away with schmaltz because Karen sold it, and *nobody* could replicate her phrasing. Decades after the singer's 1983 death, I can remember sitting in the cocktail lounge of a Maggiano's in San Jose and nearly spitting my Fat Tire beer out on the bar after hearing a Karen Carpenter tribute singer belt out the first few notes of "Rainy Days and Mondays." I was certainly impressed by the tribute singer's likeness to the late Carpenter. It was very close, yet still no cigar.

But even if C-notes were dispensing from Karen's mouth while she was singing, it would still be no excuse for the duo's horrific cover of the Marvelettes' "Please Mr. Postman" reaching the #1 spot. Yes, the attack of the nauseating oldies returns.

The Carpenters were certainly hammering away at the charts during the early 1970s, but by 1974, they were veering further and further away from the top of the Hot 100. That year, the most successful single the pair had issued was "I Won't Last a Day Without You," which just missed the Top 10. So the Carpenters were more than willing to tap into the ongoing oldies revival to rejuvenate their commercial appeal. And the hapless victim, released in November of that year, would be 1961's "Please Mr. Postman." It was the first single by Motown to become a #1 pop hit and the last #1 pop hit the Carpenters would ever score, brushing the top spot for one week in January 1975.

Aside from Karen's overly eager reading of "Please Mr. Postman"—and, not to mention, her cringy pronunciation of "lettah" and "bettah"—the backing music is terrible. The sterile and over-polished arrangement comes off like bad karaoke. And karaoke music is bad enough, which makes this music *really* bad. But in defense of the Carpenters, the Beatles didn't exactly knock it out of the park when they recorded a skip-worthy take of "Please Mr. Postman" for their 1963 LP, *With the Beatles*. Still, the Fab Four's intentions of recording the tune, as well as several other Motown cuts, partially involved getting the Detroit label's material deeper into the pop lexicon of American and English listeners. By 1975, not only was Motown a household name throughout the world many times over, but it had long since ditched the Motor City for the sunnier (and smoggier) confines of Los Angeles. Hence, the Carpenters' intention of giving "Please Mr. Postman" another go was obviously to inject more cheese into the super-cheesy pop market. And in case you haven't lost your lunch listening to the track, there's a promotional clip of the duo prancing around Disneyland in support of the single.

But what if the Carpenters put out the god-awful "Please Mr. Postman" on purpose, knowing listeners would hate it? (Don't say the duo didn't warn us about a lousy oldies comeback via their 1973 single, "Yesterday Once More.") The idea would be that if the song happened to bubble its way to the top, the oldies revival would be dead, once and for all. There's just *no* way the public could endure another "Please Mr. Postman" or "You're Sixteen." And in case you don't think the Carpenters would have dared to put out a bad record on purpose, just listen to 1977's "Calling Occupants of Interplanetary Craft" and have a nice day.

On the other hand, maybe the oldies revival had run its course by January 1975 and the Carpenters inadvertently drove the final nail into a coffin that probably should never have been pried open in the first place. After the pair had taken their rendition of "Please Mr. Postman" to the top of the charts (including those of Canada and Australia), the proverbial shark might have been jumped and the sha-la-la fun was finally over. But then again, the tune's chart-topping predecessor, Barry Manilow's "Mandy," just finished a weeklong run atop the Hot 100, so maybe the Carpenters' hit served the purpose of driving the nail into that one first.

EAGLES—"BEST OF MY LOVE" (1975)

At some point in 1975, sandpapery balladeer Tom Waits admitted, "I don't like the Eagles; they're about as exciting as watching paint dry." While the said group's most commercial output had yet to be released, Waits's summation seemed a little unfair, especially considering the Eagles had recently recorded the artist's song "Ol' 55" for their 1974 *On the Border* LP. But when it comes to the Eagles' first chart-topper, the anemic "Best of My Love," it's safe to break open a can of Sherwin-Williams.

The Eagles might not have invented country rock music, as names like Gram Parsons and the Byrds are often mentioned when that argument comes up, but the Southern California–based ensemble certainly injected country rock into the mainstream by the early 1970s. Their eponymous 1972 set, including the Top 40 classics "Take it Easy" and "Peaceful Easy Feeling," epitomized the AM radio world of jangling guitars and robust harmonies. The Americana roots of the Eagles' music is so apparent, it's interesting to know that their 1972 debut album was produced in merry old England by Glyn Johns, who had previously overseen sessions by the Rolling Stones and the Who.

The formula for the Eagles' first LP apparently worked so well, Johns was brought back for the group's follow-up 1973 album, *Desperado*. The Old West concepts heard on the sophomore effort, as exemplified by the melancholy title track, were so impressive, it might be hard for some to believe *Desperado* was a total flop, not even cracking the Top 40. As a result, the band sought to ditch their mellow typecasting for a harder rock sound and was even pointing to Johns as the culprit for *Desperado*'s lack of success. According to Johns, via his autobiography, *Sound Man*, Eagles member Randy Meisner approached the producer to convey a curious explanation: "[Meisner] told me that when he heard an Eagles song on a radio station with poor reception and interference with the signal, it did not sound very good."

Just how much acid Meisner had dropped before making the above statement to Johns is anybody's guess, but the group did meet up with the producer at London's Olympic Sound Studios (where the *Eagles* album was made) in September 1973 to lay down the track, "Best of My Love." The song was penned by Eagles founders Glenn Frey and Don Henley, along with J. D. Souther, who assisted on some of the *Desperado* material. Granted, some of the band's best harmonies are included on "Best of My Love," but you could cut the ennui brought on by the tune with a steely knife. For those aspiring guitarists who are currently taking lessons, if you form a basic C chord formation on the neck of the guitar, simply toggle your index finger on and off the B string and you have "Best of My Love."

It's clear the Eagles had intended for the ballad to be a throwaway, as they were soon off to the US to finish their third album, *On the Border*, taking "Best of My Love" with them. Hooking up with producer Bill Szymczyk at the Record Plant in Los Angeles, the group would finish the album and put onto tape the very material that would include some of the ball-busting energy they were seeking.

On the Border, released in April 1974, would spawn the bombastic rocker and first single, "Already Gone." Frey sings this piss-off anthem with so much vim and vigor that even when he tells his lover to eat her lunch all by herself, it sounds cool. But the song supposedly wasn't cool enough for the Hot 100, where the single would stall at the #32 spot. Next up was "James Dean," which employed the songwriting help of Jackson Browne (who had previously gifted the group with "Take it Easy"). "James Dean" rocks just as hard as "Already Gone" but still didn't impress enough listeners and, after peaking at #77, would crash and burn (*certainly* no pun intended).

Before *On the Border* went on the rocks, the album had one more single up its sleeve in the form of—lo and behold— "Best of My Love." The song, released in November 1974, would squirm its way to the top of the Hot 100 for one week in March 1975, making it the first of five #1 hits the Eagles would notch in its ongoing history.

Here's the official reason why "Best of My Love" became a #1 hit: outside help. Following the lukewarm success of "Already Gone" and "James Dean," a DJ from Kalamazoo, Michigan, by the name of Jim Higgs played the ballad on the air in perpetuity. Listeners managed to stay awake long enough for a nationwide buzz to be created that would nudge "Best of My Love" all the way up to the top. As mentioned earlier, the same airplay method would be effective in helping the chart-topping success of both Blue Swede's "Hooked on a Feeling" and Elton John's "Bennie and the Jets."

Here's this author's reason why "Best of My Love" became a #1 hit: sheer irony. The Eagles misjudged the next step of their career by insisting they needed to harden up their sound. But it was the very soft and mushy music style they were trying to avoid that possibly saved their asses. Sure, the Eagles would subsequently put out pop-friendly stadium rockers throughout the '70s, like "Hotel California" and "Heartache Tonight" (both chart-toppers in their own right), but who knows what would have happened had "Best of My Love" not been released and *On the Border* flopped, much like its predecessor? As for Tom

Waits's assessment of the Eagles' music, the paint might have been drying while "Best of My Love" was ascending the Hot 100, but meanwhile, its B-side—Waits's aforementioned composition, "Ol' 55"—was selling along with it.

25

FREDDY FENDER—
"BEFORE THE NEXT TEARDROP FALLS"
(1975)

B oasting one hell of a stage name, Freddy Fender might just be the poster child for what a one-hit wonder truly was during the '70s. But it was a long, strange trip before the frizzy-haired singer achieved his one and only #1 hit.

Before taking on the name of a bad-assed instrument, the musically inclined Baldemar Garza Huerta grew up in Texas as the son of Mexican immigrants. After being discharged from the Marine Corps for heavy drinking, he began making Tejano-style records in 1956 while still in his teens, taking on the Freddy Fender moniker. Unfortunately, he would score a stint in the slammer during the early '60s for a marijuana bust. For the remainder of the decade, Fender would find himself in and out of the music business before signing with producer Huey Meaux's Crazy Cajun label. It was Meaux who would suggest Fender record the insipid ballad "Before the Next Teardrop Falls," which was originally released in 1967 by country singer Duane Dee and covered soon after by artists like Jerry Lee Lewis, Charley Pride, and Dottie West. Reluctant at first, Fender recorded his own unique version of the song in 1974, adding a verse in Spanish. The tune would have enough crossover appeal to not only leap all the way to the top of the Hot Country Singles chart but also rise to the apex of the Hot 100 for one week in May 1975, making it the most lifeless single ever to do so.

Listening to Fender's take on "Before the Next Teardrop Falls," the artist articulates the bland lyrics—which involve an odd fascination with tear ducts—in a beautiful way, with a yearning that boldly displays the singer's very Tejano roots. The added Spanish lyrics is the secret ingredient that provides a sure-fire path for the song to work its way into the hearts of millions of listeners . . . the hearts of millions of *Spanish-speaking* listeners. Just how did a bilingual song shoot all the way to the top of the Hot 100? Did Fender study the freak success of the Singing Nun's 1963 all-French-sung "Dominique"? It wasn't even Christmastime yet.

The explanation behind the song's chart action might have a connection to a previous single that was sung entirely *en español* and made some noise on the American charts. In 1973, a pop group from Spain by the name of Mocedades entered their power ballad, "Eres Tú," in the Eurovision Song Contest and snagged second place. The exposure was enough for the song to make its way over to the US airwaves and climb all the way to the #9 spot on the Hot 100 in March 1974. The emotional energy of the track was just so infectious, Americans couldn't resist its charm. (The tune could be heard in the 1995 film *Tommy Boy*, at the end of the car sing-along.) Freddy Fender was certainly aware of the appeal "Eres Tú" had on the US market and must have known that if he threw in a Spanish verse on "Before the Next Teardrop Falls," it would at least separate his version from all the lousy covers that were previously made.

It was a wise gamble.

With the English lyrics intact, country fans were certainly drawn to the hefty, mustachioed crooner with funny hair, while the Spanish lyrics targeted a pop-friendly audience who didn't understand a damned word of "Eres Tú" yet still went out and bought that record or made an on-air request for the song. (Keep in mind that a decade later, Americans wouldn't be able to decipher one German word of *Falco 3*, yet that album still made its way into the Top 5.) Of course, listeners of Tejano music—who were fans of Freddy Fender anyway—gave a resounding *¡sí!* to "Before the Next Teardrop Falls," making it one of the most far-reaching chart-toppers of all time. It just would have been nice if Huey Meaux picked a different song.

It's not entirely fair to call Freddy Fender a one-hit wonder. After all, the artist would follow up his trademark hit with "Wasted Days and Wasted Nights," which, later in 1975, would sneak inside the Top 10. Although the tune would top the Hot Country Singles chart, it's possible the title of the song itself was a little too autobiographical to Fender's own sordid past and might not have had the appeal for the singer to achieve another pop chart-topper. Perhaps he should have thrown in a Spanish word or two.

26

WINGS—
"LISTEN TO WHAT THE MAN SAID" (1975)

W hen the Beatles fractured in 1970, the world seemed to be over and done for millions of adoring fans of the mop tops. But the same fans were in for some great and unfettered solo work by each former member of the group. George Harrison was the first to score a US chart-topper with 1970's "My Sweet Lord," but Paul McCartney wasn't too far behind, as he notched his first #1 on the Hot 100 in 1971 with "Uncle Albert/ Admiral Halsey," a song so freaking quirky and catchy, just the amount of thought that Paul and wife Linda put into the song made the kudos well deserving. *Ram*, the 1971 LP that "Uncle Albert/Admiral Halsey" had hailed from, is considered a solo Beatle masterpiece—loaded with plenty of subliminal jabs at ex-songwriting partner John Lennon—and a critical improvement from the four-track quality of the artist's 1970 debut album, *McCartney*.

If Fab Macca simply continued throughout the '70s using the same formula that had made both *Ram* and "Uncle Albert/ Admiral Halsey" so special, he would have been just fine and dandy. But McCartney had bigger ambitions. Employing drummer Denny Seiwell, guitarist Henry McCullough, and former Moody Blues member and guitarist Denny Laine, Paul and Linda would form Wings and release the stinky *Wild Life* at the close of 1971. While 1973's *Red Rose Speedway* wasn't much of an improvement from its predecessor, it did provide for McCartney his second US #1 hit, "My Love." After releasing the 1973 James Bond theme, "Live and Let Die"—a Top 10 hit on both sides of the pond—Wings suddenly found themselves clipped with the departure of Seiwell and McCullough. But both McCartneys and Laine soldiered on as a trio and headed to Lagos, Nigeria, to record most of the tracks for what would become the group's magnum opus LP, *Band on the Run*. Both album and title track would soar to the top of the albums and singles charts, making it a total of three #1 hits for McCartney. Something even better from Wings was sure to come.

Not exactly.

After some initial recording sessions made in London at Abbey Road Studios during the fall of 1974, Wings convened in New Orleans with new members Jimmy McCulloch (guitar) and American drummer Joe English to finish the tracks for the group's fourth LP, *Venus and Mars*. The album would feature the single "Listen to What the Man Said," a song that wouldn't even qualify as being a groupie to "Band on the Run." The stale chord progression of the tune is worsened by any discernable melody. Oh, and by the way: WHO IN THE HELL IS THE MAN, AND WHAT DID HE SAY? Is this man supposed to be God? A priest? Burt Reynolds? Gerald Ford? Paul is certainly no help with this question as he answers, "Doo-doo doo, doo-doo, doo-doo doo."

Released in May 1975, "Listen to What the Man Said" would end up at the top of the Hot 100 for one week in July of that year (just before Van McCoy took over the spot with his vague instructions on how to do "The Hustle"). If the song was supposed to represent Wings taking on the Big Easy, it hits a sour note, although Tom Scott throws in a masterful soprano sax solo.

(Maybe *he* can tell us who the man is and what exact words came from his mouth.) One thing for sure is you'll never hear the words, "Play 'Listen to What the Man Said!'" come from the mouth of any concertgoer at a Paul McCartney show today.

This is one of the entries in this book in which it's not very difficult to figure out how a certain song claimed a #1 pop ranking. Wings was absolutely on fire with ghost pepper sauce by 1975, so "Listen to What the Man Said" simply caught a whiff of the aroma. But of all the tracks on *Venus and Mars*—which is a decent album—why was that one selected? Simply put, there's not a whole lot on the LP from the pen of the McCartneys that was terribly commercial. Aside from "Listen to What the Man Said," the only other track on the album written by the happy couple that had any commercial value was the opener, "Venus and Mars/Rock Show." That song was in fact issued later in the year as a single but would peak outside the Top 10. (Perhaps American listeners were scared off by the bizarre spoken-word bridge performed by Paul in a snooty British accent.)

There is, however, one song on *Venus and Mars* that had a great amount of commercial pep but was forever left as an album track. Jimmy McCulloch wrote and sang the shuffle-rocker "Medicine Jar," an anti-drug anthem that warns of the death to come from sticking one's hand too many times inside such a jar. Interestingly, McCulloch would later contribute the similarly themed "Wino Junko" for the 1976 *Wings at the Speed of Sound* album. (What's more interesting is that McCulloch himself would tragically die in 1979 of a fatal concoction of morphine and alcohol.)

"Medicine Jar" really should have seen a single release, although it's possible if Wings put out a single composed and sung by the new guy, it might have caused some confusion out in the market as to who exactly was heading the group. It was important that the former Beatle was in the cockpit of Wings, and certainly the group could have done without any further "Paul is dead" rumors. One possible way Wings could've gotten around this dilemma was to have Paul (who does provide backup vocals on the actual track) rerecord the lead vocal on "Medicine Jar," with Linda providing harmonies while still managing to rock out on her unplugged keyboard. Instead, fans had to settle for "Listen to What the Man Said" and its immortal lyric, "Doo-doo doo, doo-doo, doo-doo doo."

JOHN DENVER—"I'M SORRY" (1975)

Yes, John. You really should be sorry.

Like Wings, John Denver was on a hot streak by 1975. Denver, born Henry John Deutschendorf Jr., occupied much of the upper echelon of the Hot 100 between 1974 and 1975. The boisterous ballad "Sunshine on My Shoulders"—which could peel the very paint that dries during a playback of "Best of My Love"—was the first in the John Denver catalog to claim the top spot, with the tearjerking "Annie's Song" following closely behind. John would get the lead out with the pretentious "Thank God I'm a Country Boy" and prove to be convincing enough with all the griddles and fiddles mentioned in the lyrics to turn that song into his third #1 hit in June 1975. The end of John Denver's chart-topping run would come three months later in the form of another ballad. A truly horrible ballad.

Overall, "I'm Sorry" is not the worst song ever written. A couple goes their separate ways, and the singer apologizes profusely for how things turned out. Fair enough. But when an apology comes for how things are going in China—in the *first* line of the *first* chorus section, mind you—that's when the sentimental mood dies faster than a Rocky Mountain high after the flashing of squad car sirens in one's rearview mirror.

While starvation and oppression are undoubtedly nothing to joke about, dopey lyrics are. The China reference could certainly be a case of Denver channeling his inner Barry ("Jump and Die") Sadler by leaving a silly lyric in place. It could be that the artist had suffered a major windsong of the brain when putting the lyric onto paper. Either way, it's tough to imagine how such an oddball song—even with a substantial amount of commercial momentum working in favor of the artist—made it to the top. There must have been some kind of divine intervention that enabled "I'm Sorry" to become a #1 hit. Seriously.

Considering how much of an odd year 1975 was for pop music, the only logical explanation for John Denver's success on the Hot 100 had to be that God was a big fan of the singer. Think about it. Denver's output was worthy of a chart-topper or two, but four? It only makes sense that a higher power (possibly the "man" Wings was referring to) had done a little tweaking of record sales and radio airplay data to ensure his favorite artist was grabbing as much of the spotlight as possible.

But why did the hits dry up for Denver in 1976? Obviously, the singer's material wasn't up to snuff by then (even the Almighty couldn't do much for a song called "It Makes Me Giggle"), but when Denver chose to star alongside George Burns in the 1977 blockbuster comedy *Oh, God!*, it was all over for the blasphemous singer. Since God is good, there was certainly no funny business from a higher power when it came to Denver's October 1997 death in a plane crash. Heck, Burns lived to be 100 years old, so both men were obviously forgiven over their roles in *Oh, God!* But since that film came out, it's clear that Denver was forever banned by the good Lord above from making any more dents on the pop charts.

Do you buy all that?

ELTON JOHN—"ISLAND GIRL" (1975)

For an artist who had made such an impact on popular music during the '70s, it's surprising to know that Elton John's very first #1 pop hit in the US wasn't his 1970 classic "Your Song." Nor was it his 1971 gift-that-keeps-on-giving ballad, "Tiny Dancer," or even his 1972 miles-high anthem, "Rocket Man (I Think It's Going to Be a Long, Long Time)." In fact, Elton's first American chart-topper would come in the form of "Crocodile Rock," a '50s-rock pastiche that managed to top the Hot 100 for three weeks in 1973 (impressively, just before all the nostalgic tripe started hitting the airwaves and record stores). In fact, Elton John had a bit of an awkward history when it came to scoring #1 hits in the US. After "Crocodile Rock" hopped and bopped off the charts, the artist's next chart-topper would arrive in 1974 via "Bennie and the Jets" (which, with the risk of sounding repetitive, had a whole lot of help from radio airplay).

Next up was a surreal John Lennon–assisted cover of the Beatles' "Lucy in the Sky with Diamonds" ringing in the new year of 1975 with a #1 placement before the Billie Jean King–inspired "Philadelphia Freedom" made it four total humdingers for Elton by April of that year. The colossal success of the future British knight was ineffable. And he was just getting started.

Before putting on his legendary Dodger Stadium concerts in the fall of 1975, Elton would issue two history-making albums. First up was the abstract and autobiographical *Captain Fantastic and the Brown Dirt Cowboy*, which hit stores in May. The LP would become the first in history ever to enter the *Billboard* 200 albums chart at the #1 spot, as helped by the gorgeous ballad "Someone Saved My Life Tonight." The tune would surprisingly only peak just inside the Top 5, but its near-seven-minute length might have had a little to do with its commercial shortcoming.

Elton, at the time, owed his record label two albums per year, so he would follow up *Captain Fantastic* with *Rock of the Westies* (a spoonerism of "West of the Rockies," a nod to Caribou Studios in Nederland, Colorado, where the LP, as well as the artist's previous two studio LPs were recorded) in October 1975. *Rock of the Westies* would give Elton the distinct honor of having the *second* album in history to enter the *Billboard* 200 at the #1 spot. And there's a whole lot of crazy shit on it. Included in the track listing is the Bo Diddley beat-driven "Billy Bones and the White Bird" and "Dan Dare (Pilot of the Future)," which sounds like a cross between "Rocket Man" and Daryl Dragon. Elton was supposedly so impressed with the result of his band's work on "Dan Dare," he insisted the tune be issued as the first single from *Rock of the Westies*, but the record label suits vetoed his wishes. The suits really should have listened.

In the run-up to the October 24 release of *Rock of the Westies*, "Island Girl" was put out as the album's leading single and would ultimately give Elton his fifth chart-topper, occupying three consecutive weeks in November. Lyrically, the song involves a Jamaican prostitute—who let's just say is described in an unflattering manner—working the streets of New York City while her boyfriend (or, possibly, stalker) pleads with her to return to the island. The controversial lyrics are in no way helped by the traces of a Jamaican dialect splattered throughout the piece. Due to its massive chart success, "Island Girl" would, throughout the years, end up on several Elton John best-of compilations, as well as appear on the artist's concert set lists until he swore it off in 1990. In 1975, "Island Girl" was deemed acceptable, but as the decades wore on, the song would become a slight PR headache for the artist, and sorry would seem to be the hardest word when it came to denouncing it. Elton did *not* need this #1 hit.

Bernie Taupin, who had penned the lyrics for virtually all of Elton John's '70s-era hits, often created works based on characters he would invent. Classics like "Levon" and "Daniel" are popular examples of this method. Some of his darker—and lesser known—character inventions include those on 1973's "Midnight Creeper" (about a serial kidnapper) and 1974's "Ticking" (about a mass shooter). Sometimes these stories would be told via the viewpoint of another disturbed character. Such was the case with "Island Girl." Unfortunately, *that* one was given the green light for a single release. This author is in no way defending the content of "Island Girl" but defends the integrity of Taupin, who wrote *for* the characters in the song, as opposed to writing a commentary *on* the characters in the song. The problem is that the very man responsible for conveying this message in the studio or onstage wore windshield wipers on his glasses. Ergo, it's easy to see how Taupin's lyrical aptitude was lost in Elton's incendiary performances.

Late producer Gus Dudgeon—who oversaw most of Elton John's '70s albums (including *Rock of the Westies*)—had proclaimed in the 2001 *Classic Albums* documentary *Elton John: Goodbye Yellow Brick Road*, "There's no such thing as a hit lyric. There are hit melodies which, if you're lucky, you'll get a great lyric to go with it." We can obviously eliminate the lyrics as being the reason why "Island Girl" quickly made it to the top. But the music is nothing to sing about either. The track is very energetic, yet it lacks a bold melody or any kind of strong chord progression (which explains why Elton preferred the melodious "Dan Dare [Pilot of the Future]" to be enshrined onto a 45 disc). When Elton and his band sing "IS-LAND-GIRL" at the chorus, it almost sounds like a childish "na-na-na" taunt. There's no trace of actual reggae music, and the driving rhythm almost sounds like "Don't Go Breaking My Heart" in training. The tune is a very interesting specimen, but it's unworthy of chart action below the Top 40 section of the Hot 100.

So how did the infamous "Island Girl" reach the #1 spot? Like Wings, Elton John was on a roll by the middle part of the '70s. But much like Stevie Wonder's "You Haven't Done Nothin'," "Island Girl" is not a very memorable song within the artist's discography (aside from its contentious history). But the one glaring attribute of "Island Girl" is the massive Hawaiian-sounding slide guitar effect Davey Johnstone plays throughout the track. If one were to question why the tune stood out so much for the suits who decided to release the song as the initial single from *Rock of the Westies*, I would point to the slide guitar licks. But as Bernie Taupin would later mention in his 2023 autobiography *Scattershot*, "The less said about 'Island Girl' the better." Let's leave it at that.

29

CHICAGO—"IF YOU LEAVE ME NOW" (1976)

Don't laugh, but Chicago was one of the most radical bands of the early '70s. With audacious anthems like the anti-war "It Better End Soon" or the seditious "State of the Union," it's easy to conclude that if Richard Nixon had heard of the group, they probably would have had some unexpected visits by the IRS. Even the titles of their albums (or lack thereof) had attitude. The group's 1969 debut LP, *Chicago Transit Authority*, shared the band's original name. But after running into some legal trouble, the group would shorten it to Chicago and christen their 1970 sophomore effort as such. Their 1971 follow-up would be called *Chicago III*, and virtually all their subsequent studio LPs would be numbered from that point on. (However, *Chicago III* really should have been called *Chicago II* . . . or perhaps *Chicago Transit Authority III* . . . or maybe *Chicago Transit Authority III, Chicago II*? Never mind.)

As fierce as Chicago might have appeared during their formative years, their hit singles were quite harmless. Tunes like "Make Me Smile" and "Colour My World" occupied the group's A-sides to become successful Top 10 hits. Even the angry 1970 rocker "25 or 6 to 4"—which managed a #4 placement on the Hot 100—lamented the perils of songwriting as opposed to draft cards.

During their early days, the creative force behind Chicago's songs was comprised of trombonist James Pankow, guitarist Terry Kath, and especially keyboardist Robert Lamm. Not only did Lamm pen the aforementioned "25 or 6 to 4," but he also wrote and sang the band's second Top 5 single, 1972's "Saturday in the Park," which really should have been a #1 hit. And getting that elusive chart-topper would prove to be a daunting task when the floor was opened for other band members to participate in songwriting duties. Trumpeter Lee Loughnane's easy-peasy ballad, "Call on Me," just edged into the Top 10, while singer and bassist Peter Cetera's own ballad, "Wishing You Were Here," stalled right outside of it. These are hardly disappointing achievements for a group, but as one of the biggest live acts of the 1970s, there must have been a sense of frustration that, while their albums had no problem shooting all the way to the top of the *Billboard* 200, none of their singles were following suit on the Hot 100.

In 1973, Chicago had begun recording their albums at Caribou Ranch studios, the same locale in Colorado where Elton John had been recording his own long-players (which means both artists might have crossed paths while Elton was putting "Island Girl" onto tape). Conveniently, Caribou Ranch was owned by Chicago producer Jimmy Guercio. And whether there was something in the water at the studio's canteen, it was at this time when the band's hits were getting a little gooey. 1973's "Just You 'N' Me"—a Pankow-penned ballad sung by Cetera—would give Chicago their third Top 5 single, while 1975's "Old Days"— another Pankow tune Cetera had taken lead vocals on—would make it a total of four for the band. Even the golden-voiced Cetera seemed to be getting a little fed up with the soft-natured themes of the group's hit material, complaining about the nostalgic "Old Days" and its cornball themes of Howdy Doody, blue jeans, and baseball cards. That's why it's fascinating that in

1976, the singer would bring to the table a song that would not only top the charts but forever dictate Chicago's soft and easy pathway forward.

With very little help from the rest of his bandmates, Cetera would assign acoustic guitar duties to Guercio for a ballad that would end *all* ballads: "If You Leave Me Now" (issued on the group's tenth effort, predictably titled *X*). With arranger Jimmie Haskell layering on strings and horns, the song would inflict a huge mellow curse on Chicago, while spanning two consecutive weeks atop the Hot 100 in October 1976. And Cetera's chums had no problems voicing their displeasure with the song. Said Lamm in Ben Joseph's *Chicago: Feelin' Stronger Every Day*, "To be sure, the 'ballad-ness' that the band became identified with through the singles after 'If You Leave Me Now'—that drove me crazy." Loughnane would further explain to A. Scott Galloway in 2003, "Walk up to anyone on any street in the world [and] go, 'Chicago,' and they'll either say, 'If You Leave Me Now' or 'Al Capone.'" Former drummer Danny Seraphine admitted in his 2010 autobiography *Street Player: My Chicago Story*, "Even after all the success it brought, I found myself still bitching and moaning about the song."

Obviously, herpes would be easier for Chicago to get rid of than "If You Leave Me Now." There was very little say among most of the group on whether the tune should have been issued as a single, as Cetera and Guercio were the only yay votes. But the two men obviously had the insight to know the song had major hit potential. And the song really is a gem, as far as its melody and structure. Its arrangement, however, makes for a great elevator ride. One would think there were just too many killer hits on the upper reaches of the Hot 100 for such a softy to hit the top. One could think again.

While 1976 wasn't quite as terrible as its predecessor when it came to pop hits, there were quite a few stinkers that dominated the top pop spot that year. In January, C. W. McCall put out a steaming turd of a single called "Convoy," exploiting the oh-so-douchey trend of CB radios that everybody was putting inside their vehicles to avoid speed traps. But the idiocy of "Convoy" pales in comparison to that of a flapping hunk of crap called "Disco Duck," which topped the Hot 100 the week before the two-week run of "If You Leave Me Now." This just might be the link.

Nobody of a higher power flips a switch to determine what pop single will grab the #1 spot of any given week (with, of course, the possible exception of "I'm Sorry"). However, Rick Dees and His Cast of Idiots' "Disco Duck" seemed to wander its way up the charts without anybody noticing. The song's one-week stay at the top of the Hot 100 was understandable, considering the times, but it was also a bit of a fluke, which means "If You Leave Me Now" was just waiting in the wings to shoot it down. So for those members of Chicago, past or present, who are still irked about the considerable success that "If You Leave Me Now" had attained, which inflicted onto the group the stigma of a kind and gentle band, just blame "Disco Duck."

30

DARYL HALL & JOHN OATES—
"RICH GIRL" (1977)

Here's a fun activity while you're sucking down beers at a tavern. If your barstool neighbors aren't raging psychopaths, ask them to name Hall & Oates's first #1 hit. Chances are, they might call out the 1982 chart-topper "Maneater." If the inebriated patrons are a little more astute, they might select 1980's "Kiss on My List," which did, in fact, hit the top of the Hot 100 during the spring of 1981. Both would be good guesses, but the duo's first chart-topper involves a tune comprised of a teaspoon of unimpressive music, a tablespoon of class warfare, and a dash of the B-word . . . and that word isn't "big," "bam," or "boom."

Long before in-house jam sessions and restraining orders, blue-eyed Philly soul purveyors Daryl Hall and John Oates were a struggling musical twosome seeking that big hit. After releasing several unsuccessful singles, the two men would score their first Top 10 hit in 1976 with "Sara Smile," a ballad borrowing liberally from the sleek arrangements heard on numerous Philadelphia International Records hits by the likes of Billy Paul and Harold Melvin and the Blue Notes, as overseen by Kenneth

Gamble and Leon Huff. Interestingly, Hall & Oates's previous label, Atlantic Records, was wary enough about the success of "Sara Smile" (issued on RCA Records) to rerelease the duo's 1973 single, "She's Gone," for yet another Top 10 hit for the duo in 1976.

All of a sudden, Hall & Oates were serious hitmakers, and their fame was becoming bigger than the both of them, so much so that their 1976 LP would be called *Bigger Than Both of Us*. The two standout tracks from the album entail the disco-drenched "Back Together Again"—outdated today, yet considerably hip for its time—and "Rich Girl," a tune that curiously chides the spoiled and affluent while implementing the same Philly Soul flavor that had encompassed previous Hall & Oates tracks.

Strangely enough, RCA had opted for "Do What You Want, Be What You Are" to be the album's leading single. It's a sluggish ballad that sounds like "Sara Smile" on quaaludes, although that might have been the point. The label could have been trying to strike gold twice with the same formula, but unfortunately, the tune would barely squeak inside the Top 40. There must have been some concern about whether "Rich Girl" would fare better as a follow-up single, considering Hall's rant about the brat in question counting on her old man's money to get by. (Hall had originally written the song about an overindulgent male acquaintance who was the son of a fast-food mogul.) The Philly Soul strut is front and center on "Rich Girl," but the track's song cycle structure just keeps the rant on repeat before Hall sneaks a "rich bitch girl" at the fade-out, much like an impish sign-off. The girl is rich. She's a bitch. So what? Good luck making a Top 40 hit out of that. The tune would reach the #1 spot by the end of March 1977 and stay put for two weeks. It would be Hall & Oates's very first chart-topper. *There's* your trivia answer.

1977 didn't exactly start out in a bitter mood, at least when it came to what was at the top of the charts. During the first week of the year, Rod Stewart was still trying to get into someone's pants with "Tonight's the Night (Gonna Be Alright)." Shortly thereafter, car wash lots became quite the hip places to hang out at while Manfred Mann's Earth Band turned Bruce Springsteen's "Blinded by the Light" into something that could very well have come from Mars.

But something else had happened during the early months of 1977. Jimmy Carter was sworn in to the Oval Office during an ongoing energy crunch reverberating throughout the US, which resulted from an OPEC embargo stemming from the 1973 Yom Kippur War. And although Carter's April 1977 speech calling for Americans to make sacrifices with their thermostats had yet to be uttered, there was certainly a feeling of indignation toward those with a bit more money in their pockets to set the temperatures of their homes down to 66 degrees. "Rich Girl" could very well have tapped into that anger. The fact that the tune remained at the #1 spot for two straight weeks meant that people were certainly ticked off at the wealthy (well, at least until ABBA's "Dancing Queen" finally chiseled it off the top of the Hot 100).

But just as President Gerald Ford wasn't able to translate Whip Inflation Now (I'm not kidding) into a "win" at the ballot box during the fall of 1976, not very many voters had much faith in Carter's anti-inflation nonsense, and the smiling peanut farmer was out on his ear in 1980.

As for "Back Together Again" (the disco-friendly track), it did find a single release shortly after "Rich Girl" fell from the top but would crap out at the #28 spot in June 1977. It was certainly a disappointment. But the magnitude of other hits "Back Together Again" was competing with on the charts at the time—including Stevie Wonder's "Sir Duke," Fleetwood Mac's Ocean Spray-licious "Dreams," and KC and the Sunshine Band's "I'm Your Boogie Man"—indeed proved to be bigger than both Daryl Hall and John Oates.

PINK FLOYD—
"ANOTHER BRICK IN THE WALL (PART 2)"
(1980)

The final few years of the 1970s gave us plenty of material on the charts to smirk about. After Debby Boone's "You Light Up My Life" took over the top of the pop spot for ten (!) straight weeks in the fall of 1977 (like a bad cold that wouldn't go away), much of 1978 belonged to anybody whose last name was Gibb. One-hit wonders like Exile ("Kiss You All Over") and A Taste of Honey ("Boogie Oogie Oogie") knew very well that their fifteen minutes of fame would have to involve a disco beat. Even the Rolling Stones put their platforms on for "Miss You," which managed a #1 placement in 1978.

1979 found the likes of Chic, Rod Stewart, Gloria Gaynor, and Donna Summer carrying the disco torch until things came to a screeching halt that summer by means of the infamous Disco Demolition Night, which took place at Chicago's Comiskey Park on July 12. Organized by local DJ Steve Dahl, the event was ostensibly set up to drive ticket sales for the White Sox, who were experiencing a dismal record halfway through the season.

But the whole affair gave fans the opportunity to bring their disco records to the park and watch them get blown to smithereens during the middle of a doubleheader between the Sox and the Detroit Tigers. "Disco sucks" was the motto of the night as participants ultimately destroyed the field, causing the White Sox to forfeit the second game. (The poor Sox also lost the first game, by the way.) The night was certainly a rough one for disco music, and the ballpark gimmick might very well have put the death knell in the genre. After both Donna Summer's "Bad Girls" and Chic's "Good Times" occupied the #1 position on the Hot 100 in the weeks following that fateful night in Chicago, disco went straight to the back of the milk carton.

The inferno that incinerated a whole lot of wax on the night of July 12, 1979, torched a lot of hot disco acts of the time. And if Pink Floyd's sole #1 hit, "Another Brick in the Wall (Part 2)," had been around during Disco Demolition Night, it probably would have been thrown into the fire as well.

Pink Floyd could hardly be considered a threat to the pop charts. Sure, the group's 1973 monumental *The Dark Side of the Moon* LP might be sitting in the record collections of every household in the world three times over, but that album's biggest commercial moment was "Money," which finished just outside the Top 10 (still impressive for a song in a 7/4 time signature). During an age where the Village People and the Bee Gees were ruling the airwaves, a prog-rock group like Pink Floyd was certainly doomed to fly away from relevancy, much like a giant pink pig. Worse yet, if that group were to release a disco-friendly single—let alone just one *part* of it—months after the destruction of such records brought down the genre, they would have been laughed out of town. But that's just what Pink Floyd did. In November 1979, the dance beat–driven "Another Brick in the Wall (Part 2)" was issued as a single and, by March of the following year, it would top the Hot 100, becoming the only single by the band to do so.

"Another Brick in the Wall (Part 2)" was plucked from Pink Floyd's 1979 double-disc concept album, *The Wall*. The brainchild of bassist-vocalist-songwriter Roger Waters, *The Wall* focuses on a fictional, mentally deranged rock star who shares the same name as the real group (further confusing people who had previously—and mistakenly—thought Pink Floyd was an actual person and were corrected). "Another Brick in the Wall," as a whole, is a suite representing Pink's early years as a schoolboy being tormented by sadistic schoolmasters. The melody is catchy and single-worthy enough, but the problem with the suite is that it's split up into several parts, making it a tough fit for one side of a 45 disc.

The following describes the entire suite in a nutshell. "Another Brick in the Wall (Part 1)," clocking in at just over three minutes, includes a first verse about someone's daddy flying across the ocean never to return (incidentally, Waters's real-life father was killed in World War II) before guitarist David Gilmour keeps a never-ending rhythm guitar vamp going. "The Happiest Days of Our Lives," which should technically be "Part 2," opens with the sound effect of a helicopter flying overhead before the full band comes in for the second verse about kids being smacked around by teachers at school. After about a minute and forty-five seconds, "Part 2" (which should be "Part 3") cuts to the rousing chorus, which is dressed up with drummer Nick Mason's disco beat and features the band and, eventually, a subversive choir of children with thick British accents railing against education and thought control (you know the lyrics) before the tune ends four minutes in with the schoolmaster screaming about meat and pudding. "Part 3" (technically, "Part 4") can be ignored, as it's merely a brief, detached section about the main character's total breakdown, using the "Another Brick" melody. Confused yet? Just be thankful I haven't brought up the argument that *The Wall*'s Disc 2 opener, "Hey You," should really be "Another Brick in the Wall (Part 4)"—or, technically,

"Part 5"—for using the same melody pattern during the instrumental bridge. Sorry about that.

The truth is "Another Brick in the Wall (Part 2)" is a confusing and incomplete story. Why in the world would people buy the "Part 2" single without any curiosity as to what happened in "Part 1"? At the start of "Part 2," the listener is immediately thrown into the chorus without warning. As funny as it is to watch someone play "Part 1" on the jukebox and develop a dumbfounded look when the tune cuts off during Gilmour's guitar vamp (just as the helicopter noise from the beginning of "The Happiest Days of Our Lives" is heard), why would a small portion of "Another Brick in the Wall" become so popular?

Pink Floyd's label, Columbia Records, was obviously more interested in selling the monstrous *The Wall* album itself rather than the "Another Brick in the Wall (Part 2)" single. After all, Pink Floyd was not a singles band, due to the extraordinary length of their LP tracks. While Columbia certainly had no issue selling copies of *Wish You Were Here* (1975) and *Animals* (1977) without any strong singles released from those albums, *The Wall*, with its steep sticker price, presented more of a challenge for the record giant's marketing department. Hence, the dubious yet straight-to-the-point "Another Brick in the Wall (Part 2)" was most likely a gateway drug designed to get listeners hooked.

And it worked. *The Wall* sold tens of millions of copies and topped the *Billboard* 200 for over a dozen weeks. In essence, the single pulled the album along like a tugboat and topped the Hot 100 while doing so. Pink Floyd—who, by that time, was imploding due to creative differences—was now hot shit. (Even director Harold Ramis initially reached out to the group to come up with the theme song for his new comedy flick, *Caddyshack*.)

With or without knowing it, radio station DJs were complicit when it came to the promotional machination behind both "Another Brick in the Wall (Part 2)" and *The Wall*. Many of these jocks would not only play the "Part 2" single but preface the track with "The Happiest Days of Our Lives," giving the listeners the whole nine yards of helicopters, verse, chorus, singing children, and pudding. With these elongated singles manufactured by DJs, nobody even noticed the disco beat on "Part 2." Well, perhaps Steve Dahl did. And, of course, this author.

the trick with "The Happiest Days of Our Lives," which he lik-
... he whole preparation of the ... ... chicken, stuffing,
... and pudding. With much ... ... table manners—
the Dickens look ... house ... ... in Oliver T-
... ... by Alfred Bec ... this ... room.

32

STARS ON 45—"STARS ON 45" (1981)

Congratulations. You made it to the worst #1 hit single of all time. Remember how I recommended in the introduction about listening to each song for yourself before reading this book? You can go ahead and refrain from downloading this one. It's total garbage.

From the ashes of Comiskey Park, disco music managed to rear its ugly head one last time in 1981 for a #1 hit that's just about as difficult to explain as it is to understand its chart-topping status. In short, "Stars on 45"—which is also the name of the credited artist—is a Dutch creation, overseen by former Golden Earring drummer Jaap Eggermont, that weaves together a medley of Beatles songs for a steady, danceable track. What had originally started out as a sixteen-minute medley was dwindled down to a five-minute trip down Fab Four memory lane, as exuberantly expressed by the multitracked vocals of Jody Pijper, who is heard lauding both disco music and the Beatles at the bookended introduction and conclusion of the edited track.

Before the first notes of any Beatles songs can be heard, the medley peculiarly begins with an instrumental snippet of the 1970 Shocking Blue chart-topper, "Venus," before transitioning into the Archies' "Sugar, Sugar" (which you'll recall from several chapters back). It's worth noting that Willem van Kooten, who ran the production company for this project, had owned the copyright for "Venus," which means someone was either trying to squeeze some royalties from the medley or Eggermont was suffering from a blackout when inserting the non-Beatles cuts into the track. But soon after the confounding "Sugar, Sugar" portion is finished, brief passages of several Beatles songs follow each other in what is a corny fusion of mop tops and polyester.

All the material heard on "Stars on 45" was reproduced by imitators and, in all honesty, they did a decent job in presenting a very impressive set of tracks spliced together. But still, why would people give two shits about Beatles impersonators in the year 1981?

Even the song title is a mess. Due to legal requirements with publishing, all songs used in the medley would have to be called out in the title for its US release: "Medley: Intro/Venus/Sugar Sugar/No Reply/I'll Be Back/Drive My Car/Do You Want to Know a Secret/We Can Work It Out/I Should Have Known Better/Nowhere Man/You're Going to Lose That Girl/Stars on 45." But because a forty-one-word title doesn't look terribly sexy on the cover of a single, the medley is more well known as "Stars on 45"—and that's how the song was listed when it claimed the top spot of the Hot 100 for one week in June 1981.

Oh, and in case I didn't mention it already, WHY WOULD PEOPLE GIVE TWO SHITS ABOUT BEATLES IMPERSONATORS IN THE YEAR 1981?

Most observers would note that John Lennon's assassination on December 8, 1980, had a lot to do with the freakish success of "Stars on 45." And it's a valid point. During the first several weeks of 1981, Lennon would posthumously earn a #1 hit with the anachronistic "(Just Like) Starting Over." George Harrison would soon put out one of the first Lennon tributes with "All Those Years Ago," which would skyrocket all the way to the #2 spot. Paul McCartney's gorgeous tribute, "Here

Today," and Elton John's somber ode, "Empty Garden (Hey Hey Johnny)," would both have to wait until 1982. But whereas McCartney's song was merely tucked away on an album, Elton's tribute to Lennon was released as a single and would manage a Top 20 placement. Lennon's death was indeed still in the headlines two years after the fact.

So it's fair to say "Stars on 45" caught a touch of the Lennon/Beatles fever that was going around at the time. But was it enough of an affliction to turn the song into a #1 hit? I don't think so, girlfriend. The answer could very well have something to do with another colossal pop single and, perhaps, a piece of obsolete technology. (And please bear with me.)

Those of us who owned a VCR back in the '80s might remember that you practically had to mortgage your home to be able to afford one. Even the hefty price tag on the movies themselves (VHS, of course) was so ridiculous that you had no choice but to stock up on the recordable tapes so you could bootleg the movies and programs off the television. Let's say, hypothetically, a certain member of a family programmed a VCR to record *The Young and the Restless* every weekday at 11:00 a.m. while she was at work, requiring the cable box to be left on the network that the said soap opera was aired on, CBS. Now, let's say a sweet, innocent child decided to watch a show on Nickelodeon while eating his Peanut Butter Cap'n Crunch cereal, just before frolicking off to school, and had forgotten to change the cable box back to CBS. Much to the horror of the family member who had returned from work to watch the recorded soap episode, nothing but a full hour of the rudimentary children's program *Pinwheel* was captured onto tape. Sure, the continuity of *The Young and the Restless* might have been slightly affected, but it soon became clear who on the show was screwing the mailman and the series went on its merry way. Analogically speaking, Kim Carnes's 1981 smash hit, "Bette Davis Eyes," was *The Young and the Restless* and "Stars on 45" was *Pinwheel*.

From mid-May until mid-July 1981, "Bette Davis Eyes" spent a total of nine weeks atop the Hot 100 (even keeping George Harrison's "All Those Years Ago" at the #2 spot). It was a huge hit that would become a perennial '80s classic. But after five consecutive weeks at the top, the tune might have worn out its welcome.

This is where "Stars on 45," which knocked "Bette Davis Eyes" off its top position for one week, comes into play.

Much like the adorable child who had mistakenly prevented one hour of *The Young and the Restless* from being recorded after getting caught up in Nickelodeon programming, listeners and radio programmers alike were caught up enough in the oddity that was "Stars on 45" to allow it to disrupt the tiresome #1 run of "Bette Davis Eyes." But the brain damage was short-lived, and "Bette Davis Eyes" would soon reclaim the spot for four more consecutive weeks. "Stars on 45" might have teased and uneased us for seven short days, but it was soon discarded into the used bin where it belongs—next to all the crappy, worn-out VHS tapes for sale.

33

BILLY OCEAN—
"THERE'LL BE SAD SONGS
(TO MAKE YOU CRY)" (1986)

You might have noticed a bit of a time lapse between the last chapter's selection and this one. The truth is one would be hard-pressed to pick a #1 hit between the years 1982 and 1985 that requires much explanation as to how it achieved its coveted placement on the Hot 100. The advent of MTV not only brought images of bad hair and crummy outfits to the households of suburbia, but its popularity provided the visual exposure artists used for the success of their singles. Unless your name was Billy Squire, MTV did wonders for performers. You could either love or hate pop sensations of the era like Madonna, Prince, Culture Club, or Dire Straits, but these acts were too ubiquitous to avoid, and it didn't take political scandals, moon landings, or any acts of God to give their songs a nudge on the charts.

As popular as rock and pop acts were during the first half of the 1980s, R&B artists were still making a lot of noise on the Hot 100. Smooth and sultry tunes like "Baby, Come to Me" (Patti Austin and James Ingram) and "Saving All My Love for

You" (Whitney Houston) had no problems peaking at the top. But one of the more excitable R&B artists to have come from this era was Trinidad-born Billy Ocean, whose contrived surname epitomizes smooth and easy; you can even smell the rancid seaweed as the artist belts out his 1985 ballad, "Suddenly."

Ocean would score his first #1 hit in 1984 with "Caribbean Queen (No More Love on the Run)." Putting aside Ocean's curious pronunciation of "Caribbean," the funk-rock-soul anthem is vintage '80s that demanded respect from those who wore either Jordache jeans or parachute pants. With both "Suddenly" and the groove-heavy "Loverboy" nearly hitting the top of the Hot 100 in 1985, the stage was set once again for Ocean to potentially grab the #1 spot with "When the Going Gets Tough, the Tough Get Going," the theme from the *Romancing the Stone* sequel, *The Jewel of the Nile*. While the sequel itself was enough to make one pass a jewel, the song should have been catchy enough to earn for Ocean that second chart-topper. But it wouldn't happen. Much like *The Jewel of the Nile*, "When the Going Gets Tough, the Tough Get Going" was a #2.

While most performers would kill for the chart action Ocean had enjoyed up until 1985, there was certainly a feeling that the singer might have peaked and was on his way down to has-been status. But nothing was further from the truth. In the summer of 1986, Ocean would somehow—and someway—achieve a smash hit that might have had a place in the hearts of soccer moms and PTA members (at least the ones outside of Harper Valley) but really had no business topping the pop charts.

This chart-topping ballad, "There'll Be Sad Songs (To Make You Cry)," has somewhat of a schizophrenic lyrical structure. In the verse and bridge sections, Ocean professes his love for someone in a way that is borderline creepy. For the sake of argument, let's just say the feeling is requited, leaving us with some very mushy lyrical content. But when the singer transitions into the chorus, he belts out the song title so matter-of-factly, it sounds as if he's breaking the fourth wall to remind (or warn) his audience what sad songs can do to their mascara. Is he talking about *this* song? Perhaps he's talking about another sad song (certainly not "Honey"). More importantly, what happened to the lady he was laying it on thick for? Is she waiting patiently while Ocean finishes his soliloquy?

The story behind the creation of "There'll Be Sad Songs" brings up even more questions than answers. One of the song's authors, Barry Eastmond, was indirectly inspired by Billy Ocean's "Suddenly" when penning the lyrics. As Eastmond explains in *Songfacts*, "[My wife's girlfriend] was at a party given by her new boyfriend and ['Suddenly'] came on and reminded her of the old boyfriend. She broke down. We thought that was an interesting story so we wrote the song about it." Not to be a stickler for details, but "I love you"—which seems to be a prerequisite for sad songs (according to the lyrics of "There'll Be Sad Songs")—is nowhere to be found on "Suddenly." But overlooking that observation, is Ocean singing about "Suddenly" when he turns to the audience for the chorus of "There'll Be Sad Songs," or is he referring to Eastmond consoling his wife's friend? Or are the lyrics about Eastmond writing about his wife consoling her friend? What the fuck is going on?

And let's talk about the contraction that is "there'll." Much like Sloopy, *there'll* is a funny little word that tends to tie tongues. But I will give Ocean a pass on this one. Just as he maneuvered around the word "Caribbean" to turn "Caribbean Queen (No More Love on the Run)" into a million-seller, he does just fine on this one.

Getting back to the question of what had compelled "There'll Be Sad Songs" to reach the top of the Hot 100, it's important to note that the song's chart-topping predecessors were major downers. From early May until early July (when "There'll Be Sad Songs" took over the top spot), the four tunes that had held the position were "West End Girls" (Pet Shop Boys), "Greatest Love of All" (Whitney Houston), "Live to Tell" (Madonna), and "On My Own" (Patti LaBelle and Michael

McDonald). So it certainly makes sense that people needed a break from depressing city scenes, wannabes, saucy secrets, and couples separating. "There'll Be Sad Songs (To Make You Cry)" just might have been the feel-good ballad to the rescue.

Ocean was also in the right place at the right time in that VH1 had just been launched and provided a platform for rock balladeers to show off their mullet-topped vocal expertise. The artist, offering his unique R&B vocal chops, just happened to be in his love zone when he became a sensual fixture on the network.

Billy Ocean was like a cat with nine lives when it came to pop music. Thanks to the 1988 Corey Haim–Corey Feldman flick, *License to Drive*, the singer would once again earn a #1 hit—his third overall—with "Get Outta My Dreams, Get into My Car." And who knows? Had he not taken a break following that feat, Ocean could very well have kept notching the chart-toppers (in two-year intervals, of course).

BOSTON—"AMANDA" (1986)

Despite a barrage of humdrum ballads, 1986 had quite a few impressive classics that reached the top of the Hot 100. While Robert Palmer's rock-heavy "Addicted to Love" will forever conjure up visions of Lilith Sternin lookalikes pounding away on fake instruments, and Prince's "Kiss" will remind us of its awful Art of Noise/Tom Jones cover put out two years later, Peter Gabriel's timeless "Sledgehammer" was duking it out for the top spot with "Invisible Touch," released by his former band Genesis. You couldn't scrape Steve Winwood's world music–flavored "Higher Love" or Bon Jovi's big-hair anthem "You Give Love a Bad Name" off the charts if you tried. Meanwhile, Peter Cetera—fresh out of Chicago—continued to apply sugar and spice to his compositions for the chart-toppers "Glory of Love" and "The Next Time I Fall."

All the above tunes had MTV (or *Karate Kid Part II*) to thank for their commercial success. If you wanted a hit during the '80s, you had to have a video for it (and a *very good* video certainly didn't hurt). But of all the #1 hits inflicted upon 1986, this author is puzzled by one entry that celebrated a two-week run at the top spot in November: "Amanda." I cannot for the life of me remember this song by Boston. If it weren't for cheesy hair-band compilations that were later advertised on TV, I'd have no idea "Amanda" even existed. I certainly cannot recall a video produced for the song. For those readers who were avid MTV couch potatoes and are wondering for themselves right at this very moment how you could have missed the "Amanda" video, never fear—your mental acuity is not failing. There never *was* a video.

That's right. Google it for yourself: no music video. In fact, "Amanda" is the last #1 single in the US not to be supported by a video. For a song to be released in the middle of the '80s without a music video yet *still* top the charts, the only logical conclusion is that it had to be one hell of tune that spoke volumes without any visual depictions. The song could only be an unforgettable antique that, to this day, brings up unforgettable memories of high school dances and pawing someone special in the back seat of a car.

Well, you would think.

Turning back the clock a bit, Boston was one of the hottest rock bands to come out of the mid-1970s. The group didn't invent arena rock but would certainly put the "album" in Album-Oriented Rock by means of their 1976 eponymous debut LP, which sold over seventeen million copies and made a whole lot of coins for their label, Epic Records. Composed and produced by guitarist-songwriter-MIT alum Tom Scholz, *Boston* has something for everyone within its grooves. If "More Than a Feeling" doesn't make you wave your hands in the air like you just don't care, you certainly have to give props to the prog-rock shuffler "Smokin'." Topping it all off are the searing vocals of Brad Delp, which would help pave the way for the success of uninhibited tenors like Mickey Thomas (Jefferson Starship) and Bobby Kimball (Toto).

While the *Boston* album was still selling copies out of record stores, the group put out their 1978 sophomore effort, *Don't Look Back*, adding even more millions of units in sales to their name. With Boston on their roster, Epic Records truly had a golden goose. And when that goose took its sweet-ass time laying another egg following the release of *Don't Look Back*, Epic started taking legal action during the early part of the '80s in order to get their million-selling artist to put out another long-player. In fact, there was an eight-year span before Boston would finally hand over their third LP, although it would be handed over to a different record label.

1986's *Third Stage*, issued on MCA Records, would boast the power ballad "Amanda," featuring Delp back on vocals belting out Scholz's lyrics, which are so mushy and gushy, it's like a Saint Bernard slobbered all over them. The emotions displayed in the song make Billy Ocean seem like a wallflower. Interestingly, someone at Epic had already put "Amanda" out as a bootleg two years earlier, which makes it perplexing as to why the tune would be picked for the lead-off single from *Third Stage*—and without a video. Altogether, Boston, MCA, and "Amanda" didn't have a wicked chance in hell for success. Yet the group—immersed in the middle of a decade overflowing with lots of neon and spandex—would notch their first and only #1 hit by means of the video-less "Amanda."

Was the novelty of MTV wearing off? Was radio making a comeback? Were the rock relics from the '70s invading the subsequent decade?

The answer to all the above questions is no, but, much to the chagrin of the Buggles, video hadn't quite killed the radio star. Evidently, radio was still a powerful enough vehicle to serve as a conduit for Boston's music to flow to the ears of fans (new and old) who, after eight years, finally got a new product from the band. Obviously, the leaked bootleg didn't hurt the commercial viability of "Amanda." But back in 1986, bootlegs only spread from hand to hand via cassette tapes, making them a very minor threat to royalties.

As for the oversentimental nature of "Amanda," there could have been a method to the madness of putting it out as a single. Like Boston, the band Foreigner cut its teeth back in the '70s with its fair share of arena rockers that never quite reached the top. It wouldn't be until 1985 that Foreigner finally scored a chart-topper with the ballad "I Want to Know What Love Is." Of course, the song had a video produced to help promote it (you know, that obnoxious video that shows the band with ear-to-ear grins when the African-American gospel singers arrive at the studio) but earned its #1 status on its own merit—you just can't help but pull out a Bic lighter when Lou Gramm delivers the climactic chorus of "I Want to Know What Love Is." Similarly, "Amanda" followed that formula and took advantage of a young generation that still took a break from the sweaty dance numbers every now and then to sway along to a slow song.

HUEY LEWIS AND THE NEWS—
"JACOB'S LADDER" (1987)

There weren't very many pop-oriented rock groups from the '80s that had the excitement and charisma of Huey Lewis and the News. Without a doubt, the Bay Area group (who seemed to make sure everyone knew they came from the Bay Area) made their indelible mark with 1983's *Sports*. The album would offer four consecutive Top 10 singles, including the MTV-friendly cuts "Heart and Soul" and "If This Is It." It's rather surprising that none of the singles issued from *Sports* had reached the #1 spot (although there was quite a lot of competition on the charts in 1983). But it was hardly surprising that Huey & Co. scored a #1 hit with "The Power of Love," the classic theme from the 1985 flick *Back to the Future*. The band was a living embodiment of hard work, fun, and great rock and roll music that kept the '80s from getting too tacky. But when the band itself started getting a little tacky and, in the case of "Jacob's Ladder," slightly out of its element, the #1s seemed to fall into their laps.

Following the success of "The Power of Love," fans became hungry for more Huey. No news was not good news. Over two years had passed since the group released a long-player, and when their follow-up LP, *Fore!*, hit stores in the summer of 1986, the same hungry fans might have asked themselves, "What's with the dumb name?" The fact that the album was the fourth to be issued by the band likely explains the facetious title, although, in comparison to *Sports*, *Fore!* was a little out in the rough.

The happy-go-lucky (and yucky) "Stuck with You" was chosen as the debut single from the group's fourth effort and would duly hit the #1 spot on the Hot 100 for three straight weeks in the early fall of 1986. Following "Stuck with You" was the infectious rocker "Hip to Be Square," which is now forever associated with someone being chopped to bits with an axe. (Don't worry, it was only Jared Leto.) Upon its original release at the end of 1986, "Hip to Be Square" should have been bound for chart-topping glory, much like its predecessor, yet settled for a #3 peak placement.

For the third single release from *Fore!*, the album's opening track, "Jacob's Ladder," was selected. The tune, filled with sleazeball evangelicals and biblical connotations, is hardly something one would think a group that came to party would record let alone put out as single. But there is a backstory. While Bruce Hornsby and the Range were recording the 1986 smash album *The Way It Is*, Lewis sat in to help with some of the production and contributed some harmonica and vocal overdubs. "Jacob's Ladder," written by Hornsby and his brother, John, was on tap to be included on the album, but the track was just not working out for the session. Hornsby had then bestowed the song upon Lewis to record with the News on their next album, which, as we know, would become *Fore!* With an over-processed production value and "splashy" drum sound, it was obvious "Jacob's Ladder" was intended as a throwaway opening track to a highly anticipated album. Still, the song was on its way to radio stations and record stores in a single format.

Why "Jacob's Ladder"? Didn't fans want to find out if Huey Lewis found a new drug? Did Huey and his crew finally start believing in love? Did the band ever finish the *Ghostbusters* theme? (Scratch that last one.)

Astoundingly, "Jacob's Ladder" would climb rung by rung all the way up to the top spot in March 1987. The only thing we can conclude is that there was yet another divine intervention in the world of popular music that benefited the chart action of Huey Lewis and the News. Hardly.

By 1986, the cassette tape had become the choice product for listeners of music. The item was easy to travel with, stick inside a Sony Walkman, or shove into a tape deck installed below the dashboard of a Pinto. But with convenience came limitations and annoyances. Aside from all the crappy tape hiss, listeners had to fast-forward or rewind the cassette for days to get to their favorite track. In the case of *Fore!*, the album's inaugural hit single, "Stuck with You," was situated as track number two, whereas "Jacob's Ladder" (as established earlier) was the first track. This meant that patient listeners were forced to endure the opener before getting to the jam. So "Jacob's Ladder" could very well have grown on listeners enough to have created a buzz for a single release of its own. Keep in mind that opening tracks had found later single releases from past albums like Michael Jackson's *Thriller* ("Wanna Be Startin' Somethin'"), Madonna's self-titled debut ("Lucky Star"), and the Cars' *Heartbeat City* ("Hello Again"). The same was true for "The Heart of Rock & Roll," an opening track that was third in line for a single release from Huey Lewis and the News' very own *Sports*. Much like those album openers, "Jacob's Ladder" had all the fixings of a Top 10 or Top 40 hit, but not a chart-topper.

This, my friends, is where the Bruce Hornsby connection comes in. The pianist was riding high with "The Way It Is," which, long before it had become a rapper's delight, topped the Hot 100 for one week in December 1986. Hence, it's not out of the question to think that more than one inquisitive listener did a little internet-less research on the composer of "Jacob's Ladder" and noticed the "B. Hornsby" credit, thus concluding,

"Oh, that must be the same Hornsby with the song about the guy in the suit who tells the homeless lady to get a job." Timing was everything.

KIM WILDE—
"YOU KEEP ME HANGIN' ON" (1987)

As the spring of 1987 was heating up into the summer, a hot dance number was certainly in order. The first two weeks of May found Cutting Crew's "(I Just) Died in Your Arms" topping the Hot 100. Once listeners upchucked their McDLTs after finding out what the group meant by "died," it was on to the next #1 hit, U2's "With or Without You." The uncharacteristically morose ballad, put out by the same group who gave us "New Year's Day" and the Martin Luther King Jr.–inspired rocker "Pride (In the Name of Love)," made a huge enough impression on suburbia that it claimed the top spot for three consecutive weeks. But soon enough, it was time to put the headbands and leg warmers on for something to sweat along to, via another '80s-era artist who hadn't caused a whole lot of ruckus in the US for the past several years.

Singer Kim Wilde scored a Top 40 hit in 1981 with "Kids in America" (which, ironically, fared much better in her native England) before being washed away into obscurity along with other short-lived new wave acts. But six years later, Wilde would reappear on MTV with an explosive, catchy dance number that seemed to have #1 hit written all over it: "You Keep Me Hangin' On." As a ten-year-old kid (in America), I found the song quite impressive after catching the music video depicting Wilde belting out the song in a room equipped with a high-powered fan blowing debris and blond hair all over the place. Considering its strong melody and overall construction, the song deservedly achieved a #1 ranking on the Hot 100 for one week in June 1987. Wilde's six-year absence from the US charts could only mean the singer spent all that time crafting a song that was sure to be one of the greatest products to come out of the '80s, right?

Fast-forward six or seven months. The successful Robin Williams flick *Good Morning, Vietnam*—based on real-life US Air Force disc jockey Adrian Cronauer, who served during the Vietnam War—was just released onto VHS, with a copy finding its way into my family's living room VCR (when the device wasn't being used to record over soap operas). While watching the movie, I distinctly remember the hyperactive Williams sticking shrimp heads on his fingers and singing "You Keep Me Hangin' On." I might have only been ten years old, but I was smart enough to know that a song that most recently lit up dance floors accentuated with neon strobe lights seemed awfully out of place in a movie based in the year 1965. I soon learned the song was originally recorded in 1966 (a less egregious anachronism) by the Supremes, and it shot all the way to the top of the charts that same year. And once I heard the Supremes' original version, one thing was clear between the original recording and Kim Wilde's rendition: BOTH SONGS SOUND EXACTLY THE SAME.

Sure, on Wilde's version, about sixty thousand more volts of electricity is used for the multitudes of synthesizers heard on the track, but the core of the song is unchanged. Many other artists throughout the years had covered "You Keep Me Hangin' On," with rock outfit Vanilla Fudge achieving the most success, taking their sedated version to the Top 10 in 1967. So how could a pop singer take an electronic clone of the song back to the top of the charts over twenty years later?

Couple of things. First, there's the Supremes angle. In 1982, Phil Collins would score his first Top 10 hit in the US with a cover of the Motown trio's hit "You Can't Hurry Love," which, like "You Keep Me Hangin' On," had also topped the Hot 100 in 1966. And, as with Kim Wilde's cover of the latter, there was nothing spectacularly unique about Collins's take on "You Can't Hurry Love." The fact is the Supremes were still well loved in the 1980s. This was fantastic news for the bank accounts of the authors of their hits, Brian Holland, Edward Holland Jr., and Lamont Dozier, as well as for the chart action of unlikely pop stars from across the pond who could successfully convey their own renditions—namely Wilde and Collins. (By the way, Phil, don't wander off too far—you're up next.)

Secondly—and most importantly—tricked-out versions of oldies seemed to be in vogue at the time, the most notable example being Bananarama's cover of the Shocking Blue's 1970 chart-topper, "Venus" (as touched on in the "Stars on 45" entry), which, in 1986, would become the first and only #1 hit for the British triad. Not only was Bananarama's treatment of "Venus"—with synthesizers a-blazing—markedly different from the garage-band sound of the Shocking Blue recording, but their performance almost mirrors a scene at a Saturday night slumber party of high school girls. Aside from all the tea that was spilling about Jimmy getting caught passing a note in class or how Brenda is such a slut, you can easily imagine the girls busting out in unison with full-throated vocals into their hairbrushes when Bananarama's "Venus" comes on the radio. The point is, younger people related to the latter cover. So it might not be too crazy to say that Ricky Wilde—brother of Kim and producer of "You Keep Me Hangin' On"—took some pretty good notes when the "Venus" remake came out.

It's also important to note that artists from the '80s did have to choose their oldies covers carefully. Australian pop phenomenon Kylie Minogue would dig up Little Eva's 1962 chart-topper, "The Loco-Motion"—which Grand Funk Railroad would impressively take to the #1 spot again in 1974—for a 1988 synthed-up remake. Minogue's cover of "The Loco-Motion" would peak inside the Top 5 but fail to make it a third trip to the top for the artifact. And that might have been the issue: Whatever in hell the so-called Loco-Motion dance was (which pretty much sounds like a rip-off of the conga line) might have seemed too fatuous, even for the fatuous '80s.

As for "You Keep Me Hangin' On," it's fair to say Diana Ross was not too wild about her former group's hit climbing back up to the top of the charts in the mid-1980s. Her lack of any feedback of the cover leads us to believe she either didn't fancy the Casio-enriched renovation of the tune or she was just too flattered and choked up to make an effusive statement about it. Okay, the latter theory might be unlikely, and Ross simply could have thought a masterpiece should be left alone and unmolested. (Anybody up for "Ain't No Mountain High Enough"?)

PHIL COLLINS—
"A GROOVY KIND OF LOVE" (1988)

Get this. In the fall of 1988, the UK was rife with scandal as *Buster*—a movie loosely based on British crook Buster Edwards, who participated in the 1963 Great Train Robbery— was drawing major receipts at theaters all over England. The country's moral fabric was in danger of being pulled apart as Brits everywhere were fuming over a film that was seen as glorifying a criminal. Things were so dire that pop star Phil Collins, who played the lead role in what would be his big screen debut, personally reached out to Prince Charles and Princess Diana and advised them not to attend the premiere (as a scandal involving the Royal Family would just be unthinkable). *Buster* eventually topped the box offices in England, making it one of the most controversial British flicks to do so.

In the UK, *Buster* was a big deal. In the US, nobody gave a rat's ass about the movie or, for that matter, even knew who in the hell Buster Edwards was. (He could have been on the Los Angeles Dodgers' injured reserve list along with half the team.) In fact, *Buster* couldn't even rake in a million bucks following its September 1988 release in America. It was a flop. But in all fairness, the timing of the film's US debut wasn't exactly impeccable, as it came out at the tail end of a summer that gave us major blockbusters such as *Who Framed Roger Rabbit* and *Die Hard*. Still, the notion that not one but two (!) songs from the *Buster* soundtrack would reach the top of the Hot 100 would seem against all odds. But this author is certainly not handing out a pack of lies, as two *Buster* singles would indeed reach the top spot. And one of them should never have done so.

With and without Genesis, Phil Collins was a major player in the pop world during the '80s. The singer and drummer would score a total of seven solo chart-toppers in America. (His final #1 hit, 1989's "Another Day in Paradise," holds the distinct honor of being the last US single to top the Hot 100 at the end of the '80s and first to do so at the start of the '90s.) So Collins—who is a decent actor—clearly had the star power to carry a small-budget movie like *Buster*. Of course, Collins's involvement in the film would be twofold in that he could also supply the soundtrack. But since *Buster* was set in the '60s, the challenge for the artist would be to record selections that would fit in with the zeitgeist of the era. In other words, "Sussudio, Part 2" wouldn't work.

One of the songs Collins recorded for the film was "Two Hearts," a '60s throwback that enlisted the songwriting assistance of Lamont Dozier (who we'll remember coauthored the Supremes' "You Keep Me Hangin' On," among many others). "Two Hearts" had so much of a Motown vibe yet was constructed with modern elements (without too many cheesy synthesizers), which made it feel right at home during the late '80s. The tune, which was the second single released from the *Buster* soundtrack, would climb all the way to the top of the Hot 100 for two straight weeks in January 1989. "Two Hearts" certainly had a quirky flair to it, yet its #1 status was well earned. It's the previous single that's the problem.

For the first *Buster* single, Collins had ventured deep into the vaults of the '60s. Wayne Fontana and the Mindbenders hit the scene during the British Invasion with the oddball 1965 single "The Game of Love," a #1 hit in the US that settled at the #2 spot in the UK. Later in 1965, a Fontana-less lineup of the Mindbenders would release the ballad "A Groovy Kind of Love," cowritten by Carole Bayer Sager, who would later collaborate on hits with future hubby Burt Bacharach. The song's clunky arrangement entails basic guitar licks, abrasive backing vocals, and a military snare drum pattern that is a little reminiscent of that heard on "Ballad of the Green Berets" (without the jumping and dying). Despite its idiosyncrasies, "A Groovy Kind of Love" would become a #2 hit in both the US and the UK. Collins was supposedly impressed enough with the Mindbenders's hit to apply his own special touch for an all-new recording. But what listeners got was something they could have listened to with Tom Waits while watching paint dry.

About a month before *Buster* had hit theaters—and just before Michael Dukakis started driving his tank all the way to 111 electoral votes—"A Groovy Kind of Love" was released. In the place of the Mindbenders' original haphazard arrangement is a sluggish version drowning in keyboards and strings, with Collins drowsily blurting out the lyrics. By October 1988, a month after *Buster* came and flopped in the US, "A Groovy Kind of Love" found itself atop the Hot 100 for two straight weeks. How could a boring single from a movie nobody watched do so well?

Another personal story might help to clear things up. Decades ago, your favorite author knew how to play a chord or two on the piano. At the same time, he was a working stiff employed in the advertising office of a major retailer in San Francisco. His piano playing impressed one of his coworkers enough—we'll just call her Maria—that she asked him to learn and play "A Groovy Kind of Love" at her wedding reception during her and her husband's first dance. In the run-up to the wedding, this piano virtuoso asked Maria if she preferred the

Mindbenders' original recording of the song or Phil Collins's cover version, to which she replied, "Oh, I thought it was *only* a Phil Collins song."

BINGO!

The fact is Phil Collins was such a superlative '80s pop star, it's easy for people to believe that each and every song he recorded was composed by means of his own pen. (Hell, many listeners probably thought Collins wrote "You Can't Hurry Love.") And despite its subpar recording history, "A Groovy Kind of Love" is a very nice song. It's so nice that fans simply accepted the singer's sluggish cover as a reimagining of his languid 1985 chart-topper "One More Night."

The remarkable thing about Phil Collins's remake of "A Groovy Kind of Love" is that listeners seemed to look past (or possibly even embraced) the term *groovy* in the song title. The word certainly fit in with the timeline of *Buster*, but those who were buying records in 1988 didn't exactly have '60s-era platitudes like *groovy* in their vernaculars (unless they were making fun of *Brady Bunch* reruns). But one thing was for sure: Along with both Tiffany and Billy Idol covering Tommy James and the Shondells ("I Think We're Alone Now," "Mony Mony") and George Harrison tipping a hat to James Ray ("Got My Mind Set on You"), Phil Collins's nod to the Mindbenders' "A Groovy Kind of Love" continued a yearlong trend of male artists from a bygone era getting their second wind with new and improved upgrades of their hits. Well, at least new ones.

MICHAEL DAMIAN—"ROCK ON" (1989)

When you can't go with the times, go retro.

1989 was a year saturated with some truly depressing hits. Clones of past oldies from yore were replaced by ballads so shiftless and mournful, they made the slow hits from 1970 seem like high-octane numbers one would find at a rave. Sure, R&B artists like Bobby Brown ("My Prerogative") and Paula Abdul ("Straight Up," "Forever Your Girl," "Cold Hearted") did break up the monotony of gloom that was resonating at the top of the charts, but when Poison first burst our bubbles in January 1989 with the downer "Every Rose Has Its Thorn," who would have thought the song would be a harbinger of thorny themes to come?

While Mike + the Mechanics advised us to hug our fathers before they're six feet under ("The Living Years"), former *Kids Incorporated* star Martika warned us to avoid the dope or we would all drop dead ("Toy Soldiers"). And even after they got their men, Debbie Gibson ("Lost in Your Eyes") and the Bangles ("Eternal Flame") were *still* bawling over spilled milk. Madonna's controversial chart-topper, "Like a Prayer," was certainly made for teens to dance the Cabbage Patch along to at high school dances, but the song's lyrical themes were dreary enough to cause everyone to weep into their cans of Pepsi. What in the world was going on in 1989?

Considering what was topping the Hot 100, it was only a matter of time before someone broke the emergency glass and recorded a corny cover song. But rather than escaping back to the groovy '60s, some artists stopped off at the early '70s for their material. In July, Simply Red scored a #1 hit with Harold Melvin and the Blue Notes' "If You Don't Know Me by Now," which topped the R&B charts and landed in the Top 5 of the Hot 100 seventeen years earlier. Simply Red's chart-topping cover was a bit surprising, but keep in mind the song had played nonstop on VH1 and in the lobbies of dental offices everywhere shortly after its release. About a month before "If You Don't Know Me by Now" enjoyed its weeklong run at the top, an unlikelier hit would reach the #1 spot by an unlikely pop star by means of a song that was largely forgotten.

Back in 1973, British actor and singer David Essex released "Rock On," a trippy, groove-laden song that celebrates blue jeans, summertime blues, pretty girls, and Jimmy Dean (James Dean). Essex had starred in the 1973 throwback film *That'll Be the Day* alongside Ringo Starr and—being an aspiring rocker himself— had written "Rock On" for the purpose of it being played during the end titles. The producer of the film rejected Essex's song for being a little too off the wall. (Whether it had anything to do with producer's decision-making process, it's worth noting the melody of "Rock On" has a striking resemblance to that of Ringo Starr's 1972 single, "Back Off Boogaloo.") But Essex's despondency didn't last very long, as he would score a solo record deal and release "Rock On" as a single that would become a Top 10 hit by March 1974. Meanwhile, a young aspiring rock star from America was taking note.

As a kid, when this author wasn't taping over episodes of *The Young and the Restless* (I mean . . . whoever that was), he noticed a young mullet-clad actor on the show that every girl seemed to like. His character's name was Danny, and he was given the opportunity to sing on several of the episodes. Michael Damian, who played this character, scored his day job on *The Young and the Restless* after being seen by CBS execs performing on *American Bandstand* in 1981. But the actor did not give up his rock star dreams and, along with his rock star moments on the soap opera, would record a synth-loaded version of Essex's "Rock On" in 1988, with all electronic bells and whistles implemented. The recording would gain traction after being included in the 1989 Corey Haim–Corey Feldman film, *Dream a Little Dream*, and would race all the way up to the top of the Hot 100 in June of that year.

It seems that the success of Damian's rendition of "Rock On" had all the markings of serendipity: pop music meets Hollywood. Even better was the fact that the two Coreys were hot and in very high demand in Tinseltown. Dream on.

Yes, when the two Coreys first appeared together in 1987's *The Lost Boys*, they were inseparable box office draws. The duo's legacy was seemingly solidified with the 1988 film *License to Drive*, which pulled in over $20 million at the box office. But *Dream a Little Dream* was a flop, barely making over $5 million. Nonetheless, "Rock On" reaped the rewards from its exposure in the movie and topped the charts. Confused? Join the club.

In short, "Rock On" was a cover of a Top 10 hit from generations ago, recorded anew by a singer and actor who took his rendition—which was included in the soundtrack of an unsuccessful film—to the #1 spot. (Sound familiar?)

Michael Damian was a talented performer, but Phil Collins he was not. Therefore, star power alone could not have helped "Rock On" grab the top spot. Damian might have also been a dreamboat, but he was certainly no Uncle Jesse, and even Uncle Jesse couldn't score a hit, with or without the Rippers. Nothing was too corny for the '80s, but when Damian advises the kids to "rock and roll" and "rock on" while strutting his stuff—as opposed to the laid-back, ironic sneer of the chorus hook presented by Essex for his original 1973 release—not a whole lot of

kids were nodding their heads along with the soap star's recording while making devil horns with their hands.

So just how *did* Damian's "Rock On" stand out and earn
a #1 showing smack dab in the middle of 1989? Did I bother to
mention the year was loaded with some *truly depressing hits*?
Danny boy just happened to buck the trend.

SWEET SENSATION—
"IF WISHES CAME TRUE" (1990)

A new decade was upon music fans, which meant new and exciting things were (hopefully) on the horizon for an ever-changing pop world. The '80s gave us new wave, yuppie rock, and tackiness to the nth degree, with MTV and lots of keyboard-based toys leading the way in promotion and innovation. It was a silly time but, for the most part, an enjoyable one.

So what was in store for the '90s? More technological advances? Would aging pop stars (e.g., Bruce Springsteen, Tina Turner, Billy Joel) find a welcoming home in the coming decade, as they did during the '80s?

As if. Soon enough, it would become abundantly clear that if your rock music didn't involve flannel shirts and power chords, you'd probably get a mucus-filled spitball projected your way. Similarly, if your favorite hip-hop group didn't follow the nihilistic, sample-happy ways of gangsta rap, someone might have busted a cap in that group's kente-patterned threads.

But before all that fun started—and just before *Billboard* changed the way it pulled radio airplay data and record sales for its Hot 100 rankings—soft and gentle singles were (thankfully) starting to lose their grip on the charts. In 1990, Janet Jackson had two chart-toppers with the dance-friendly "Escapade" and rock-friendly "Black Cat." Madonna taught us how to strike a pose with "Vogue," while New Kids on the Block notched a doozie with "Step by Step," a song that moved a hell of a lot faster than their previous hits. Alannah Myles's gritty and sexy "Black Velvet" turned out to be a wonderful anomaly after it had become a #1 hit, and even Jon Bon Jovi looked cool when he notched his own solo chart-topper with "Blaze of Glory." And then there's Vanilla Ice, who was the first rapper to take a hip-hop single to the top of the Hot 100 with "Ice Ice Baby" . . . um, we won't go there.

The energy was indeed picking up on the charts at the dawn of the new decade, but the gooey stuff was still festering. Before becoming a slow-pitch softball legend, Michael Bolton took up three weeks at the #1 position of the Hot 100 with "How Am I Supposed to Live Without You," a song he had cowritten and originally given to Laura Brannigan several years earlier for an adult contemporary single. Taylor Dayne ("Love Will Lead You Back") and Roxette ("It Must Have Been Love") had taken their sob stories to the top, while Wilson Phillips broke onto the scene with . . . um, we won't go there, either. But the #1 status of a particular song from 1990 is so bewildering, it's a thing that could make anyone go hmm.

Sweet Sensation was a New York–based, all-female trio that formed during the mid-1980s. Despite the competition with many others of a similar template, the group, led by Betty LeBron, would forge ahead in search of that big hit. After struggling to break into the Top 40, Sweet Sensation finally did so by the close of the '80s with "Sincerely Yours" and "Hooked on You." A remake of the Supremes' "Love Child" followed in 1990 and would become the trio's highest-charting single up to that point, peaking at the #13 spot. (As we've recently learned, you could not go wrong with Supremes covers in the '80s.) In

September 1990, however, the ladies would reach the top of the Hot 100 with what has got to be one of the most nondescript ballads of all time.

"If Wishes Came True" is comprised of a tired, my-baby-left-me-and-I-wish-he-would-come-back theme heard about a million times before in countless weepers (and nobody even plants a tree and dies in this one). While the title would serve as an inspiration for the themes of many proms and winter formal dances across the country, the song itself is so generic and, considering the number of decent tracks that were starting to make some headway on the charts in 1990, a little embarrassing to listen to. Even if the members of Zack Attack heard "If Wishes Came True," they probably would've said, "Wow, we'd sound like total pussies if we recorded this."

Sweet Sensation's reign at the top would last for only a week, but it was a week too long. Sappy was fine, but "If Wishes Came True" could lather every single tree in North America. Its success must have been a sweet mistake, right?

If you look back on the history of some of the all-female R&B/dance acts to have come out of the '80s, you will notice somewhat of a trend. The fast songs were popular, but the slow numbers gained the most commercial mileage. For example, Klymaxx scored a breakout hit in 1985 with "Meeting in the Ladies Room," but it was "I Miss You," from that same year, that really took off and provided the Los Angeles ensemble a Top 5 hit. Since 1986, Exposé had been heating up the charts with sweaty cuts like "Point of No Return" and "Let Me Be the One," but it was 1987's "Seasons Change" that struck a chord and gave the trio their first and only #1 hit. Sweet Sensation followed this trend of releasing dance singles that were so-so, but when things slowed down, it was make-out time and the ballad was on its way to the top.

Sweet Sensation rubbed the genie's lamp just in the nick of time, as the '90s were about to get a little dirty and awfully ugly; after all, it's a little hard to imagine the girls belting out "If

Wishes Came True" above a mosh pit or as the opening act for Snoop Dogg (although both scenarios would've been quite entertaining to see).

It's fair to say Sweet Sensation was the last of the teeny-bopper Mohicans from the '80s, which was the final decade in which Top 40 radio—along with old music industry standards—was used to help determine who was and wasn't a pop star. Yes, cheesiness would continue to make its mark on the charts (and it continues to this very day), but the hits would become more and more predictable and less and less interesting to talk about.

"TO BE WITH YOU"—MR. BIG (1992)

I f Sweet Sensation represented the final '80s girl group act to dazzle at #1 with synthesizers and neon miniskirts, Mr. Big was the last group with big hair and musical aptitude to achieve a chart-topper. All the while, the music industry was getting turned upside down on its axis.

In 1991, *Billboard* made a giant technological leap in how it compiled data for its Hot 100 listing. Rather than wait for record stores to report their sales figures, Nielsen SoundScan would be used to pull the transaction of each compact disc and cassette purchased the very moment each unit was rung up at the counter. For radio airplay data, gone were the days of prodding Top 40 stations to provide their statistics regarding what was on rotation. BDS (Broadcast Data Systems)—a new technology that enabled airplay data to be quickly pulled from a wide range of radio stations—would become the official tool *Billboard* would use to track airplay, twenty-four hours a day. Sound fair? Au contraire.

By the time the '90s came around, single record sales were becoming a thing of the past. The kids were shelling out beaucoup bucks on full-length CDs, and the record companies knew it. One of the biggest hits of the start of the decade, MC Hammer's 1990 smash "U Can't Touch This," was only released as a twelve-inch vinyl single for disc jockeys to spin on their turntables. Hammer's label, Capitol Records, had banked on the unshy rapper's full album, *Please Hammer Don't Hurt 'Em*, selling like hot cakes. And the risk paid off, as the CD would sell over ten million copies, while "U Can't Touch This," lacking a cassette or compact disc single release to the stores, would squeak just inside the Top 10 before floating away in its parachute pants. (The same gamble would pay off years later with No Doubt's "Don't Speak," which never had any single format release.) This practice of record companies pushing full-length CDs as opposed to the singles, caused plenty of problems with the ability (and eligibility) of songs to make any noise on the Hot 100.

The advantage disc jockeys had with fewer singles and more full-length CDs lying around the radio stations is that it would become easier for them to dictate what was more single-worthy from a twelve-track digital product on which the songs can be skipped. This was the case with Mr. Big's feel-good chart-topper, "To Be with You." Atlantic Records had chosen a tune called "Green-Tinted Sixties Mind" as the leading single from the California-based glam metal band's 1991 sophomore set, *Lean into It*. But the jocks had other plans and played the hell out of the acoustic "To Be with You," which closes the album, until the suits at Atlantic had no choice but to issue the track as its own single release. Accompanied by an MTV video showing the members of Mr. Big—including lead singer Eric Martin and former David Lee Roth bassist Billy Sheehan—either straddling chairs or clapping hands while donning ear-to-ear smiles, "To Be with You" would reach the top of the Hot 100 at the end of February 1992 and spend a total of three consecutive weeks at that position. It's hard not to feel warm and fuzzy over a bunch of dudes with long hair and ripped jeans singing a hopelessly optimistic anthem for the love of a girl whose father likely wouldn't approve of the length of their wavy locks. "To Be with You" is a highly enjoyable song that deserves its chart success . . . that is if the clock was turned back a few years.

In case you missed it the first time, "To Be with You" topped the Hot 100 a couple months into 1992. By that time, Pearl Jam had released its breakout debut, *Ten*, while Nirvana had a baby's ding-a-ling swinging in every record store across America via their breakout release, *Nevermind*. Hypercolor was out and flannel was in. So why in 1992 would listeners care so much about a ballad by a group of guys more fit to be huddled behind a gymnasium between classes, sharing a pack of Camels?

Much like Sweet Sensation, Mr. Big arguably caught the tail end of the relevancy of their genre. "To Be with You" was undoubtedly propelled by somewhat similar smash hits released the year before by Extreme ("More Than Words") and FireHouse ("Don't Treat Me Bad"). Mr. Big simply caught the last slice of pie. And considering the fact that the band would enjoy years of success overseas in Asia—while being shunned in their native US—timing was everything.

One other thing that could have been a factor in the #1 status of "To Be with You" has to do with the song's chart-topping predecessor. For three straight weeks before the reign of "To Be with You," a different song jam-packed with enough haughtiness to put New York, Japan, and cats to shame had occupied the top spot. Yes, the dreadful "I'm Too Sexy" by Right Said Fred both delighted and frightened us as the cold winter months were coming to a close. However, after three weeks US record consumers might have found themselves too sexy for a quirky, pompous-assed dance track and headed straight for the spandex. In turn, three weeks of "To Be with You" might have been too much to bear for pop fans who turned to Vanessa Williams for the uber-sugary "Save the Best for Last" for five consecutive weeks. Five *looooong* weeks.

SNOW—"INFORMER" (1993)

Back when I was sixteen or seventeen years old, I spent a lot of time at my cousin's house out in the country. Most of the trouble we got into involved playing heated games of *HardBall!* on Sega Genesis or riding an ATV around the property and scaring cattle. But one trip out to the country will forever be stored in my memory bank.

I'm not exactly sure what led up to this incident, but I found myself standing outside the house and below the window of my cousin's upstairs bedroom. For whatever reason, he flung a compact disc in a Frisbee motion down at me. Being a quick thinker, I immediately saw the silver projectile coming my way and attempted to block it with my hand. The piece of plastic—which is intended to provide a lifetime of pure listening enjoyment—succeeded in slicing open the side of my hand, just below the pinky finger. The injury by no means warranted a 911 call, and, honestly, I was more impressed with the physical damage a seemingly harmless round object could do. But what I distinctly recall was the name of the artist that was printed on the disc. When I retrieved the CD to determine what unlucky performer was expendable enough for someone to play a mildly violent prank, I noticed it was credited to someone by the name of Snow. Before I started writing this book, this hand-slicing incident pretty much represented the extent of my knowledge of this artist.

White hip-hop artists might have gotten a bad rap throughout the years. However, with the exception of the mockery leveled at the Beastie Boys or Eminem, much of this ridicule has been understandable. When hip-hop music hit the suburbs back in the '80s, much of the rapping done by those who weren't exactly from the streets mostly came off as parodies for use on answering machines, hip-hop dance instructional videos, or shitty high school talent shows. White rappers were indeed frowned upon. White reggae artists, on the other hand, have somehow been given a free pass. Elvis Costello's "Watching the Detectives" was just another cool track off his 1977 debut LP, *My Aim is True*. The Police used self-deprecation to address the trend in the form of the name of their 1979 sophomore set, *Regatta de Blanc* (translation: "White Reggae"). Just because pale young men from England could make reggae work, it certainly couldn't work for someone similar looking from Canada, eh?

Ladies and gentlemen, I give you Snow.

Toronto-born Darrin O'Brien had grown up in a portion of the city that had a heavy Jamaican immigrant population. Given the nickname Snow (for obvious reasons) by his neighbors from the Caribbean, O'Brien was influenced by both dancehall reggae and hip-hop music as the '80s progressed. Teaming up with New York–based producer M. C. Shan, Snow would cut "Informer" in 1992. The hip-hop-reggae-fused track was inspired by a 1989 incident Snow was facing trial for in Toronto involving two counts of attempted murder. After "Informer" was pressed and set for release on the artist's *12 Inches of Snow* CD (again, named for obvious reasons), Snow would be acquitted of the attempted murder charges but sent to prison for a lesser assault charge. And while Snow was pounding out license plates behind bars, "Informer" would, between March and April of

1993, spend a total of seven consecutive weeks at the top of the Hot 100. And no, that was not a typo.

What was America thinking? Seven straight freakin' weeks?

To explain the success of "Informer," some listeners might have the inclination to point a finger at Vanilla Ice and his own chart-topping success with 1990's "Ice Ice Baby." Did America drop that zero only to get with another zero? Probably not. Yes, as noted earlier, Mr. Ice holds the honor of owning the first hip-hop track to top the Hot 100 (don't look at me), but it was only for a weeklong run and, by 1993, the song—and, for that matter, Queen's "Under Pressure"—was ancient history.

One valid reason for the #1 status of "Informer" has to do with The Box, an all-request music video channel that existed during the early '90s. With The Box, listeners could pay—by means of dialing a 1-900 number—to request a wide range of videos that weren't on heavy MTV rotation. (This explains why the Puppies' "Funky Y-2-C" became a Top 40 hit.) The "Informer" video was a mainstay on The Box, thus allowing the single to circumvent MTV exposure and "licky-boom-boom-dem" itself all the way to the top of the charts.

It's also worth noting that, by the spring of 1993, people were having a serious case of Whitney Houston Fatigue from fourteen straight weeks of "I Will Always Love You" dominating the charts. Adding insult to injury, after Houston's highly success-ful run at the top was halted in March 1993, the sap-fest con-tinued with the Peabo Bryson–Regina Belle duet "A Whole New World," from the Disney cartoon feature *Aladdin*, claiming the position. But "A Whole New World" would be locked inside the vaults forever after just one week at the top of the Hot 100. So, in a way, Snow and his rap-reggae swagger was a sight for sore ears.

Still, what's with the seven-week run?

Look no further than UB40. In 1983, the mostly Caucasian British reggae ensemble put out a cover of the 1967 Neil Diamond single "Red Red Wine," gaining some modest suc-cess in the UK. When the song was released five years later in the US, it would become a massive sensation. Believe me, I was there. *Everybody* loved the song. *Everybody* played it on their tape decks. UB40's energetic reggae rendition of "Red Red Wine" would reach the top of the Hot 100 for only one week in October 1988, but keep in mind there was a lot of competition in the form of chart-toppers like Bobby McFerrin's "Don't Worry, Be Happy," the Beach Boys' "Kokomo," and—you guessed it—Phil Collins's "A Groovy Kind of Love." By the early '90s, Americans were thirsting for more Anglo-reggae hits, and Amy Grant's "Baby, Baby" just wasn't doing the trick. "Informer," however, gave listeners dance, rap, and—most importantly—pop-crafted reggae.

If you need more proof of the UB40 connection, look no further than what happened in July 1993. Almost five years after topping the charts with "Red Red Wine"—and just a few months after "Informer's" chart run (and roughly around the time of my minor hand injury)—UB40 would strike lightning again in the form of a reggae-juiced version of the 1961 Elvis Presley hit "Can't Help Falling in Love." The tune was featured in the William Baldwin–Sharon Stone film *Sliver* and, like "Informer," would spend a total of seven consecutive weeks on top of the Hot 100. And it had nothing to do with the false hope that someone was once again going to cross her legs without wearing panties.

LOS DEL RIO—
"MACARENA" (BAYSIDE BOYS MIX) (1996)

I know you have two very important questions to ask right about now: "Why is 'Macarena' sashaying into my brain again?" and "What did I do to deserve such torture?"

Sure, you thought "Macarena" was dead and buried with the rest of the '90s and not worth a graveyard exhumation, even as the subject of a book that questions the validity of the chart-topping nature of certain hits. But considering all the changes pop music was enduring throughout the early '90s involving the de-emphasizing of single sales and the new method of how radio airplay was being pulled (while keeping in mind that music piracy was still limited to the one guy on the block who had a CD burner), it should come as no surprise that, as the decade progressed, the top of the Hot 100 was being occupied by some questionable hits. (I mean, Boyz II Men are a fine vocal group, but thirteen goddamn weeks at the top with "End of the Road"?)

1996 was arguably the smelliest year of the decade when it came to pop chart action. R&B and hip-hop had become major fixtures on the Hot 100 during the early portion of the '90s, thanks in part to alternative music being confined to the Modern Rock chart. But the finger singers were on fire by 1996. Songs by Mariah Carey, Celine Dion, and Toni Braxton collectively took up twenty-four weeks (!) of the #1 spot that year. So when two guys who looked more like air conditioner repairmen instead of pop singers came out with a tune that topped the Hot 100 in 1996—becoming one of the chart's longest-running singles in history—it seemed as if the skating rinks were getting ready to open in hell.

The story behind "Macarena" is a complicated one, but the gist of it is that Los del Rio—made up of Spanish flamenco–pop vocalists Antonio Romero Monge and Rafael Ruiz Perdigones—originally put out "Macarena" (without the electronic pizazz we all recognize) in their native Spain in 1993. A couple years later, a Miami-area DJ took the record to his buddies—better known as the Bayside Boys—to spruce it up into a club-friendly remix. By the summer of 1996, the song was at the top of the charts, inspiring lousy, uncoordinated dancers everywhere to do the "Macarena" at wedding receptions, baseball stadiums, and political conventions.

"Macarena" would spend a total of fourteen consecutive weeks atop the Hot 100 from August to November 1996, annoying the living shit out of just about everyone. To give you an idea of how long this timeline was, a few weeks into the song's chart-topping run I moved into a sweltering apartment in the Silicon Valley with four roommates who had big dot-com dreams. By the time "Macarena" fell off the top, I was using their overheated computer monitors to warm my freezing hands after coming home from a minimum-wage warehousing shift at Marshalls clamping security tags onto imitation Tommy Hilfiger shirts.

Even after the tune strutted its way off the number position, it would linger on the chart, notching a total of sixty weeks on the Hot 100. To some, "Macarena" was a sick joke that disturbed the continuum of forgettable hits from 1996. It contained a pulsating beat that gave these disgruntled listeners epileptic seizures and severe cases of stomachache every time they saw the hands of amateur dancers go out, behind the head, and then down to the hips.

To others, "Macarena" was just what the doctor ordered. Following a string of ho-hum singles that had come out in 1996, it seemed that, once again, pure excitement and hype was—at least temporarily—the determining factor of auspicious chart action on the Hot 100. In a big way, these people saw "Macarena" as something that was flipping the proverbial bird to *Billboard*'s new format and the new promotional ways of record labels. The song's success was a beautiful joke that most cynics could only wish would last until the end of the millennium.

Consider this author in the latter camp. Bravo, amigos.

WILL SMITH FEATURING DRU HILL AND KOOL MOE DEE—"WILD WILD WEST" (1999)

One of the greatest visual products to have come out of the '90s was *South Park*. The animated series—created by Colorado buds Trey Parker and Matt Stone—has successfully slain every obnoxious aspect of pop culture and politics for the past few decades. Some of the show's best content came out in 1999, during its third season, including a three-part series called "The Meteor Shower Trilogy." On one of the three episodes, "Two Guys Naked in a Hot Tub," the 1999 Cher hit "Believe" is lampooned. In a nutshell, the adult characters get together for a party, which the ATF mistakes for a cult gathering and tries to force them out by blasting "Believe" (which is re-created in a garbled mess of electronics and moaning) at high decibel levels in front of the house. The ATF's plan turns out to be futile, as the adults are already grooving out to "Believe" while inside.

In another of the trilogy episodes, "Cat Orgy," Eric Cartman (the big-boned child character who manages to annoy everybody) has a newfound obsession with the 1999 Will Smith summer flick *Wild Wild West* and dresses up in full-on shades-clad cowboy garb while rapping his own version of Smith's theme song from the movie. Cartman's rap entails a lot of gibberish, as he describes—in sparse, "wiggy-wiggy" detail—of saving Salma Hayek from metal spiders alongside his partner Artemus. It's a complete train wreck, yet it's not much worse than the actual Will Smith song.

There's no doubt that, by 1998, Smith was a major threat on both the silver screen and in the studio. 1997's *Men in Black* was a monster draw at the box office and was arguably responsible for the multiplatinum success of the rapper-slash-actor's 1998 *Big Willie Style* album, which not only featured the chart-topping "Gettin' Jiggy Wit It" (including a sample of the 1979 Chic hit "He's the Greatest Dancer") but also had Smith's titular theme song from *Men in Black* slipped into the track listing. As a song, "Men in Black" is one strange puppy, implementing the less-than-memorable 1982 Patrice Rushen track "Forget Me Nots" into the chorus hook. With an accompanying music video showing Smith dancing around with animated aliens, it seems that if the tune got any cornier, you could sell oceans of ethanol. Still, although it didn't chart at all on the Hot 100 (more on that in a bit), "Men in Black" succeeded in making its way onto everyone's portable CD player.

Fast-forward to 1999. Will Smith, Kevin Kline, and Salma Hayek would star in *Wild Wild West*, which resurrected the '60s-era sci-fi/Western TV show of the same name for the big screen. The film would count on lots of special effects and a bit of slapstick (pardon the pun) for its appeal. *Wild Wild West* would find Smith once again returning to the studio to record a rip-roaring title theme song, utilizing a sample of the 1976 Stevie Wonder track "I Wish." Also appearing on "Wild Wild West" is vocal group Dru Hill (yes, it's more than one guy) and rapper Kool Moe Dee, for what would become a weeklong chart-topper for Will Smith in July 1999. Considering the notoriety of *Men in Black*—both film and song—it would only make sense for the artist to keep his jiggy momentum going for yet another #1 hit.

The problem is, whereas *Men in Black* was a blockbuster, *Wild Wild West* was a heaping pile of horse manure. Granted, the movie had Austin Powers, Jar Jar Binks, and the sniffling faces of *The Blair Witch Project* to compete with, but it even struggled to recover its own $170 million budget. As for the theme song, "Wild Wild West," it's just awful. Perhaps the tune is not *quite* as awful as the Escape Club's 1988 chart-topper of the same name—which pillages from Elvis Costello's "Pump It Up" like an outlaw—but awful just the same. Smith raps about he and Artemus saving Salma Hayek presumably from metal spiders (sound familiar?) while the nauseating chorus refrain— as rapped and sung by Moe Dee and Dru Hill (respectively)— can only veer moviegoers away from the theater entrance of *Wild Wild West*'s showing and into the entrance of *Lake Placid*. (Hmm . . . maybe *that's* why *Lake Placid* did so well.) 1999 was going through a serious pop music facelift in the form of Britney Spears and Ricky Martin, as well as a major comeback from guitar wiz Carlos Santana, so there was certainly no reason for listeners to give a shit about how Will Smith was continuing to get jiggy wit it toward the close of a millennium.

There sure was.

Like most successful artists and impresarios of the hip-hop world, Will Smith is brilliant. Going back to the mid-1980s, when rappers such as Run-DMC, the Beastie Boys, and LL Cool J were sampling (or flat-out reconstructing) mainstream pop and rock hits for their own recordings, people ran out and bought them in mass quantities. Sean "Diddy" Combs can speak for himself when it comes to his freak-off parties, but he knew damned well what he was doing when he practically pirated the Police's 1983 chart-topper "Every Breath You Take" for "I'll Be Missing You," the rapper-slash-producer's tribute to the late Notorious B.I.G., which spent eleven straight weeks at the top of the Hot 100 in the summer of 1997.

But as much of a rip-off as "I'll Be Missing You" might be, look at what Coolio did with "Gangsta's Paradise," which took up three consecutive weeks of the Hot 100 in September 1995. Not only did Coolio liberally use Stevie Wonder's 1976 track "Pastime Paradise" as the structure for "Gangsta's Paradise," but he completely rewrote the song for its inclusion in the *Dangerous Minds* film.

Smith must have known the jigginess would continue in both record sales and chart action if he added a slice of Stevie into his music. But using "I Wish"—which, like "Pastime Paradise," was pulled from Wonder's 1976's monstrous *Songs in the Key of Life* set—was a bold decision. Whereas nobody under thirty had really heard of "Pastime Paradise" before it was nicked for "Gangsta's Paradise," causing too many foolish listeners to believe Coolio had come up with the keyboard riff all by himself, "I Wish" went straight to the top of the Hot 100 in January 1977. Luckily for Smith, the move would pay off. After all, more people took Diddy's "I'll Be Missing You" seriously than those who laughed their asses off after noticing a copy-and-paste job of Andy Summers's first dozen guitar notes. So it's safe to say Stevie Wonder's '70s-era magic had rubbed off on "Wild Wild West" as it did a few years earlier on "Gangsta's Paradise." (It's even safer to say the composer was paid handsomely for signing off on both tunes.)

Getting back to the earlier *South Park* references, one could say there was a battle going on between Cher's "Believe" and Will Smith's "Wild Wild West" when it came to the charts in 1999. (Trey Parker and Matt Stone surely knew what they were doing when they selected both songs as audio punching bags.) While "Wild Wild West" represented the usual rap braggadocio fans had been accustomed to for the past fifteen years, "Believe" relied heavily on Auto-Tune to catapult a fifty-two-year-old singer back to the top of the Hot 100 (and for four straight weeks, mind you). It wouldn't be long before every artist and their grandmother would lather Auto-Tune onto their voice for hit singles.

It's also worth mentioning—and not just because I said I would get back to "Men in Black"—that before 1998 had come to an end, the *Billboard* Hot 100 updated the way it ranked singles, including airplay-only songs that did not necessarily have a commercial release. With this new guidance, "Men in Black" easily would have climbed to the top of the chart based on the similarly titled film and—recalling a few chapters back—"U Can't Touch This" would have earned for MC Hammer a #1 hit. But this new radio airplay ruling, along with several other factors to be discussed, would ultimately contribute to the Hot 100 becoming its very own Wild West.

44

LONESTAR—"AMAZED" (2000)

Country music, twenty-first-century style.

The fleeting weeks of 1999 were a very concerning time. Sure, people weren't exactly diving out of windows or emptying their bank accounts, but the threat posed by two simple digits were certainly on everybody's mind. It was the Y2K bug. Fortunately, the lanyard-wrapped dot.com soldiers figured out how to get '99 to change over to '00 peacefully so that financial institutions wouldn't melt down and cashiers at Hot Topic could still ring up Sublime T-shirts on New Year's Day of the new century.

But soon enough, less merchandise would be rung up at record stores. With online piracy sources running wild on the information superhighway, in the form of file-sharing services like Napster, Gnutella, and Kazaa, grannies everywhere were amassing their Andy Williams tunes by a simple click of a mouse as opposed to bothering with a trip down to the mall. Record stores everywhere were putting up their going-out-of-business signs, with the Wherehouse being one of the first major retailers to shutter its doors during the early part of the decade. Tower Records' 2006 bankruptcy, however, would effectively drive the final nail in the coffin of a recorded product with an MSRP listing on its cellophane. (With, of course, the exception of vinyl records, which weirdos still shell out big bucks for. Ahem.)

To keep up with a brave new world of music, artists needed to get even more creative with their appeal. And crossing over into multiple genres is always a great way to gain new audiences. Country music artists perfected this practice throughout the '90s. During the early part of that decade, Garth Brooks would rope the country genre in the wind and dump it onto the mainstream, whether the mainstream liked it or not. (Even this author still has *The Chase* in his collection.) But although Brooks has a gazillion chart-toppers on the country charts—and plenty of #1 albums on the *Billboard* 200—his singles never reached the top of the Hot 100. Simply put, Brooks didn't release any of his material as pop singles. The Hot Country Songs chart is where the artist preferred his hits to simmer and never bothered releasing or promoting them as pop singles (well, except for when it came to that goofy Chris Gaines thing).

As the '90s progressed, crossover country stars like LeAnn Rimes, Shania Twain, and Faith Hill would take a stab at getting that elusive #1 hit on the Hot 100, but all would come up short. Even Billy Ray Cyrus and his fantastic mullet would stall at #4 with 1992's "Achy Breaky Heart" (and no, I don't have that one in my collection). In fact, the last song to have topped the Hot 100 from the country genre was the 1983 Brothers Gibb creation "Island in the Stream," recorded by Kenny Rogers and Dolly Parton. I say "country," although "Islands in the Stream" has about as much twang in it as a Marilyn Manson song. Individually, Rogers and Parton had achieved their greatest chart action with the pop-centric singles "Lady" and "9 to 5" (respectively). Hence, if a country artist wanted to land atop the Hot 100, the song would have to absolutely hit it out of the park. It would have to be either a major toe-tapper or a timeless ballad that, for years to come, would be requested by both sentimental pop and country listeners and serve as the soundtrack to countless weddings and karaoke set lists.

Enter Lonestar. The Texas-bred outfit had bounced around for a while in Nashville during the early '90s—with Big & Rich's John Rich plucking the bass in the lineup before splitting in 1998—and did score a handful of Top 10 hits on the Hot Country Songs chart, two of which, "No News" and "Come Cryin' to Me," would both reach the #1 position. But armed with a super-sweet ballad called "Amazed" (penned by Nashville songwriters Chris Lindsey, Aimee Mayo, and Marv Green), everything would change for Lonestar. Recorded for their 1999 *Lonely Grill* album, and helped in no small way by the emotional lead vocal work of Richie McDonald, the group was ready to kiss the bride. They found their wedding song.

"Amazed" would top the Hot Country Songs chart in 1999 and slowly wiggle its way into the pop side of the music world, topping the Hot 100 for two weeks in March 2000. The song represents a perfect blend of pop and country sensibilities, so it's easy to see why it had such an effect on both charts. After all, the chart-topping run of "Amazed" on the Hot 100 followed that of tearjerkers by Savage Garden ("I Knew I Loved You") and Mariah Carey–Joe–98 Degrees ("Thank God I Found You"). "Amazed" simply found a warm and snuggly home on the pop charts.

That more than explains why "Amazed" became a #1 hit. So what's my beef?

This author is not here to bust the balls of any song that might have suffered a slight overdose on gushy, lovey-dovey subject matter (that is, unless the song is directed at persons by the name of Honey or Sloopy). But if the verses of Bryan Adams's "Please Forgive Me," the chorus of Aerosmith's "I Don't Want to Miss a Thing," and the introduction of Seal's "Kiss from a Rose" had a baby, it would be "Amazed" (in a weird threesome kind of thing). In fact, every time my ears meet "Amazed," I not only think the song sounds like 1993's "Please Forgive Me," but I keep wondering if it *is* "Please Forgive Me" and Lonestar simply forgot the rest of the song after the verse. So why did no one seem to pick up on the similarity between the two songs and suggest, "Hey, maybe we should make an edit to this and that"? Furthermore, how come no legal action was taken?

Indeed, rather than ask, "How did this shit become a #1 hit?" the more appropriate question for this chapter is, "How did nobody get sued?"

Country music has had a long history of borrowing a piece of this and that from other works. Just compare Johnny Cash's 1955 classic "Folsom Prison Blues" to Gordon Jenkins's "Crescent City Blues," released two years earlier. Sun Records owner Sam Phillips reportedly told Cash to pay no mind to the legal matter of the stark similarities between both songs, although the Man in Black would later be forced to cough up $75,000 in damages.

The case of the Cash tune was far more egregious than that of "Amazed," but maybe—just maybe—there was a little inside baseball involved in "Amazed." "Please Forgive Me" was composed by Bryan Adams and producer Robert John "Mutt" Lange. Many will not only remember that Lange, formerly married to Shania Twain, was highly instrumental in his then-wife's run of hits during the late '90s but that he and Adams had penned the 1997 Lonestar single "You Walked In," which reached a respectable #12 on the Hot Country Songs chart. Could the songwriters—or perhaps their publisher(s)—have eased up on the copyright of "Please Forgive Me" in favor of "Amazed" being issued as a single? Could there have been a financial agreement between all songwriters involved? Does no one else hear the likeness between both tunes? Maybe Adams and Lange haven't even heard "Amazed" yet. You never know.

45

DESTINY'S CHILD—
"INDEPENDENT WOMEN" (2000)

By the close of the twentieth century—after all the Spice Girls nonsense was dead and buried—a far more exciting "girl power" group was born. Destiny's Child followed in the same ilk as predecessors En Vogue and TLC, but with trickier vocal structures and a far more modern R&B sound tailor-made for the twenty-first century. Of course, Beyoncé Knowles would prove to be the Sting of the hill and move on with a highly successful solo career that still gets bigger and bigger with each passing minute. But while the nerds were working on the Y2K bug, Destiny's Child was everywhere. They were the *true* Spice Girls. Whereas "Bills, Bills, Bills" would claim the top of the Hot 100 for a weeklong run in July 1999, "Say My Name" was far more exciting. Striking fear into the hearts of men who were even thinking of cheating and had a limited number of minutes on their Motorola Timeports, "Say My Name" would take up three consecutive weeks of the #1 spot in the spring of 2000 (incidentally knocking Lonestar's "Amazed" off the position).

Destiny's Child was so in demand by 2000, it only made sense for the makers of the November 2000 big-screen revamp of *Charlie's Angels*—starring Drew Barrymore, Cameron Diaz (pronounced "dee-azz"), and Lucy Liu—to utilize the musical trio in support of the three stars of the film. (Interestingly, Destiny's Child started out as a quartet but had dwindled down to a triad by late 2000 following a whirlwind of lineup changes.) The song chosen for the film would appropriately be titled "Independent Women."

Reworked as "Part 1" for the soundtrack, "Independent Women" is smart. It's got beats. Even I could get jiggy wit it. As for the film itself, *Charlie's Angels*, released on November 3, 2000, was a pretty decent blockbuster draw, domestically bringing in $125 million on a $93 million budget. It was able to stick around in theaters until subsequent preholiday flicks like *How the Grinch Stole Christmas* and *What Women Want* ate into the movie's box office mojo.

Meanwhile, "Independent Women," released ahead of *Charlie's Angels* in August, would find itself at the top of the Hot 100 by the week of November 18, just after the film hit theaters. But then something strange happened. November turned into December, and "Independent Women" was still the uninterrupted #1 single. And then—wouldn't you know it?—as America was ringing in the New Year of 2001, the song *still* wouldn't come off the top. As each week of January went by, "Independent Women" remained at the top of the Hot 100. Finally, during the first week of February 2001, it would be dethroned—eleven weeks later—by Shaggy's "It Wasn't Me." By then, *Charlie's Angels* was a thing of the distant past. (It *was* you, Shaggy. You broke our hearts.)

Do I think "Independent Women" deserved its #1 status? Absolutely. But for eleven straight weeks? Not a chance. The song is no "Bills, Bills, Bills." It's certainly no "Say My Name." In fact, "Independent Women" outperformed the combined chart-topping run of both said singles by nearly threefold. So could people have been too distracted by the end of 2000 to care about what was lighting up the Hot 100? Throw up those hands.

The distraction theory could be explained by the following three factors: George W. Bush, Al Gore, and the Beatles.

First, the politics. On November 7, 2000, Americans went to the ballot box after months of a long, grueling—and obnoxious—presidential campaign season. It all came down to one night and, just before 8:00 p.m. EST, Gore was declared the winner of Florida's twenty-five electoral votes by several media outlets, almost assuredly paving the way for the sitting vice president to claim the Oval Office. But *did* he win Florida? Just after 2:00 a.m. EST on November 8, it was determined that enough votes were found to put Bush ahead in Florida. Bush was now the declared winner of the White House, and Gore had the humiliating task of calling the Texas governor to congratulate him. But not so fast. Just two hours later, the Florida count was determined too close to call and officially declared undecided. Gore now had the awkward task of calling the Texas governor to take back his concession. Thus, over the next month, a headache of recounts, lawsuits, butterfly ballots, and hanging chads would plague the nation.

Many voters pointed to the media's inaccurate calls on election night as the reason for their anxiety. After all, as former NBC anchor Tom Brokaw described it in *Newsweek*, "We don't just have egg on our face—we have an omelet all over our suits." Still, the election fiasco made for great television. But all good things must come to an end and, on December 12, the US Supreme Court nixed a statewide hand recount request and Bush was declared the winner. No suits would require any dry-cleaning this time around.

It's easy to see how people might have cared very little about what was on top of the charts during this nerve-wracking period, leaving free reign of the Hot 100 to Destiny's Child. But what about *after* December 12? That still leaves about seven weeks left of the #1 chart run of "Independent Women."

This is where the Fab Four come in.

Just when you thought you were done picking up every *Anthology* volume by the Beatles—whether it be the six audio discs or the colossal documentary on VHS (or DVD, if you were more refined)—a 368-page book was dropped into bookstores in October 2000. What was special about this book was that it was comprised entirely of interviews (past and present) of all four members of the Beatles and pieced together chronologically so the reader could experience, word for word, every minute of the band's journey. (I should know; I read all three hundred thousand words of the book while everyone was still screwing around with the Florida vote count.)

But what was even more special was the release of Beatles *1*, a remastered collection of all the group's #1 hit singles (yes, even "Paperback Writer") on one CD. The album had hit record stores in early November, roughly around the time "Independent Women" rose to the top spot of the Hot 100, and would reach the top of the charts in two dozen countries and ultimately sell tens of millions of copies. And its timing was impeccable, being that Christmas was just weeks away. So, if you didn't feel like wrapping an awkward four-pound book to place under the tree, a three-ounce compact disc served a better purpose (and was cheaper). The CD would indeed be the big seller as the final weeks of 2000 were winding down, and its sales would continue into the New Year, considering everyone who still had a $20 Sam Goody gift card to part ways with.

The Beatles *1* compilation has been deemed the biggest-selling album of the first decade of the new millennium. Considering that recorded music would soon become a free-for-all for all on cyberspace, this stat isn't entirely surprising. And any remastered product by the Beatles was big news in 2000, since the band's studio recordings were still mostly only available in their crappy, hiss-filled digital versions from the '80s. It really is amazing for an album to do so well without a single release, as each of the twenty-seven tracks included had already lived on a 45 disc from decades earlier. So this obviously left an opportunity for an act to take up the #1 position on the Hot 100 for weeks and weeks on end. Especially if that act at the time was the hottest female vocal group in America.

46

JAMES BLUNT—"YOU'RE BEAUTIFUL" (2006)

History repeats itself. Just like this author had some difficulty finding selections from the first half of the '80s to feature in this book, he was equally stumped when trying to pluck something that topped the Hot 100 during the early portion of the 2000s. But this was certainly a different time. Illegal file sharing was replacing CD sales at an alarming rate, and the suits at the record labels couldn't figure out how to combat the practice. All the FBI warning stamps in the world couldn't terrify the listening public out of amassing illegal downloads—after all, as a digital pilferer, the worst thing that could happen to you was being featured in a Pepsi Super Bowl commercial. Metallica and Dr. Dre would famously go after Napster for P2P (peer-to-peer) sharing and, ultimately, the service would shut down after a judge had ordered them to keep track of their download history in relation to the copyrights of the songs.

But the damage was done. There were far too many other Napsters on the dark web to stem the P2P flow. Hence, as record stores were going belly-up, the countless number of record labels that aspiring rock stars had once filled up the wasted baskets of with their demo tapes were quickly becoming reduced to three conglomerates: Universal Music Group, Sony Music Entertainment, and Warner Music Group.

So, with a lack of A&R presence in the record business, it should come as no surprise that music had become quite homogenized by the early 2000s. Or was it the "Oh-Ohs"? Or was it the "noughts"? Some even refer to the decade as the "noughties." Either way, the #1 hits were certainly of a naughty and sweaty nature as the decade was making its way through an industry in ruin. R&B and hip-hop artists like Usher and 50 Cent were dominating the charts with up-tempo hits, making the Hot 100 look more like a dance party than a respectable source that once proclaimed "Mr. Custer" as a legitimate chart-topper. But why shouldn't the Hot 100 be a dance party? Isn't music supposed to make people feel good and want to dance? Sure. But when Outkast enjoyed a nine-week run at the top with 2003's "Hey Ya!"—which blends the likes of rock, pop, and *Pac-Man*—it was clear that listeners were longing for a break from the norm. And this could help to explain why James Blunt's 2005 ballad, "You're Beautiful," slowly but surely topped the Hot 100 as well.

Being an English singer-songwriter, the odds were clearly stacked against Blunt in his pursuit of the top position of the American pop charts. If the noughties were all about busting a move on the dance floor, nobody from across the pond was invited. And while Blunt's fellow compatriot Dido did come close with the Top 5 2001 hit "Thank You," Eminem's sampling of the tune for 2000's "Stan" was the contributing factor to this feat (as opposed to the lyrical notion of tea getting cold). With the Beatles being several years away from remastering their entire catalog for what would turn out to be a salvo of reissues that continue to this very day, the Brits had to do something overly exhilarating to top the US charts. It would have to be something that would send the asses of Molly-loaded clubgoers out to the dance floor. It would have to be something naughty and sweaty. Instead, it would be the kind of tune one would hear while slipping out the back door of the club for some fresh air.

"You're Beautiful" is kind of like the "Ben" of the new millennium. Composed around the subject of a lost love, it's a gorgeous song that might be too gorgeous for chart-topping status. The song is also too soft for anything else that other male artists were releasing at the time. And the video—which portrays Blunt deciding whether he wants to commit suicide or make out with the camera—doesn't help matters. Released in the spring of 2005, "You're Beautiful" made quite a bit of noise in Europe and Australia before making its way over to North America in the fall. In March 2006, the tune would finally reach the top of the Hot 100, but not before some not-so-soft tunes like "Laffy Taffy" (D4L) and "Grillz" (Nelly) claimed the position. "You're Beautiful" would have to halt the five-week run of Beyoncé's "Check on It" for its own one-week run in March . . . and no contentious elections or Beatles compilations were anywhere to be found.

It's easy for one to conclude that people were longing for some kind of break so they could get outside for some fresh air, and "You're Beautiful" might have been that very slow song to provide a lull on the charts. But Blunt's song seemed to connect with listeners and could very well have inspired subsequent chart-topping ballads like 2006's "Bad Day" (Daniel Powter) and 2007's "Hey There Delilah" (Plain White T's) to follow suit. With *Billboard* still a year away from including streaming data into their chart rankings, the success of "You're Beautiful" is nothing short of remarkable. But there might be one more twist to the plot.

In the original recording of "You're Beautiful," Blunt drops a doozie when singing about being "fucking high," although the lyric was edited to "flying high" for the single's radio release. This is somewhat reminiscent of the 1974 Raspberries ballad "Starting Over," on which lead singer Eric Carmen recalls being "so fucking optimistic" in the first line of the song, as his lovely piano chords flow along. You can easily miss the word in the Raspberries tune if you pick your nose, but, in a way, the brevity of profanity almost pushes away the listener who gets a little too close to the song for an embrace.

However, whereas "Starting Over" was never released as a single, both Steve Miller's 1977 rocker "Jet Airliner" (which mentions "funky shit") and Radiohead's 1992 Cobain-lifter "Creep" (which blurts out "so fucking special") were. And both tunes would respectively end up reaching the Top 10 of the Hot 100 and Hot Rock and Alternative Songs charts. Of course, the bad words were removed from each song for commercial use, but whenever they're played on an online radio station or in someone's Uber, anyone familiar with either song can't help but wonder if they're getting the clean or potty-mouthed version. In other words, the f-bomb in "You're Beautiful" might have been a selling point. (Using an expletive to sell a product? The nerve!)

This chapter represents another example in which the expletive in the book's title *doesn't* apply to the song itself. "You're Beautiful" is certainly not shit, but for the music era during which it had topped the Hot 100, it awkwardly stands out, much like the lack of a space in between Justin Timberlake's "SexyBack." It's safe to say that James Blunt's "You're Beautiful" makes for some very *good* shit—it just needs to watch its fucking mouth.

MAROON 5—"ONE MORE NIGHT" (2012)

After the naughty noughties had winded down, something weird began to happen on the *Billboard* Hot 100: Everybody seemed to be growing up. In hip-hop, the debauchery at the club was being replaced by more serious subject matter, like Jay-Z's "Empire State of Mind," which took up the #1 spot for the last five weeks of 2009. The next year, newcomer Bruno Mars—via his first chart-topper, "Just the Way You Are"—showed everyone there was more to dance music than just booty and drugs. (Incidentally, both mentioned tunes are *not* Billy Joel covers.) On the singer-songwriter front, British songstress Adele scored two chart-toppers in 2011 with "Rolling in the Deep" and "Someone Like You." All the while, our lives truly would have sucked without pop stars like Rihanna, Lady Gaga, and Kelly Clarkson.

In case you didn't notice from above, female artists were taking up a lot of real estate on the Hot 100 and deservedly so. But even some of the male-dominated rock groups were making their marks; this includes Foster the People, whose #3 hit, "Pumped Up Kicks," could have arrived on a time machine from an '80s teen movie, and Fun, who took up six straight weeks of the top spot in the spring of 2012 with the Janelle Monáe–sung

"We Are Young," a tune one could imagine Freddie Mercury singing at Live Aid (in between all his "ay-ohs").

But one of the most exciting rock acts of the time was Maroon 5. The Southern California group, which mixes a potpourri of influences in their charismatic sound, has been dazzling the charts since 2002, via the Top 40 groover "Harder to Breathe." "This Love" and "She Will Be Loved" would edge into the Top 5 in 2004, before "Makes Me Wonder" gave the band their first #1 single in 2007. ("This Love" is a *far* better track than "Makes Me Wonder" and should have been their first chart-topper, but whatever.) By the end of the decade, Maroon 5 had moved further and further away from the Top 10, but they would roar right back into it after joining forces with pop superstar Christina Aguilera for 2011's "Moves Like Jagger" (#1) and rapper Wiz Khalifa for 2012's "Payphone" (#2).

Front man Adam Levine would become a superstar in his own right in 2011 after being offered a spot on the panel of *The Voice*. And it's hard to argue that Levine's presence on the show had, in turn, helped to maintain Maroon 5's presence on the charts. Even the fact that the group would upgrade to a sextet in 2014 (in contrast to the digit in their name) was amusing enough to give them some good press. But very little could explain why a cow pie of a song called "One More Night" could dominate the Hot 100 for nine consecutive weeks. But this author is up for the challenge.

Yes, from the end of September 2012 until the close of November 2012, "One More Night" would outlive a presidential election, Hurricane Sandy, and binders full of women. Do you remember "One More Night"? Sure, the Phil Collins tune that hit the top of the charts in 1985, right? No, but somewhere Collins is reading this chapter and asking, "Hey, jerk—how do you like my 'languid' ballad now?" Overseen by Swedish pop producers Shellback and Max Martin, "One More Night" could best be described as an overproduced reggae track and a far cry from past megahits Martin was responsible for, including Britney

Spears's ". . . Baby One More Time" and Katy Perry's "I Kissed a Girl." In a way, "One More Night" harkens back to the puzzling success of 2000's "Independent Women." The difference is the former is just not a good song at all. There's no empowerment and very little booty-shaking.

If my theory about the chart-topping success of Snow's "Informer" is correct, the same might apply to "One More Night." America loves its Anglo-reggae, and Maroon 5 was there to provide the fix, although this was likely unintentional on the part of the band. Max Martin's intentions could have—and I stress *could have*—been a different story. Of the many artists the songwriter-producer has worked with, Swedish pop darlings Ace of Base was one of them. The group's hits, "All That She Wants" (1992, #2) and "The Sign" (1993, #1), had surefire reggae beats. But what kept the kids from taking Ace of Base seriously as a reggae ensemble—and this is coming from someone who was still lathering Clearasil on his face and running to make his first-period chemistry class while the group was still on the radio—was the fact that they were seen as ABBA impersonators as opposed to Jimmy Cliff impersonators. But Martin—who, in all fairness, did not start working with the quartet until their biggest hits had fizzled off the US charts—must have known the group had a good thing going with that processed reggae beat. And, with rock outfits like 311 later incorporating reggae into their material (for better and *horribly* worse), the market for Anglo-reggae was not souring anytime soon. Therefore, if the point of unleashing "One More Night" to the world was to capitalize on this market, it was nothing short of brilliant . . .

On the other hand, according to the ancient Mayans, the world was supposed to end on December 21, 2012, so it's possible everybody was just too busy prepping to give a rat's ass about what was on the charts.

ROBIN THICKE FEATURING T.I. AND PHARRELL—"BLURRED LINES" (2013)

Okay, this one might be set up for me on a tee-ball stand. When the subject of Robin Thicke's 2013 chart-topper, "Blurred Lines," arises, what usually comes to mind are images of gratuitous sex, borderline bestiality, and some model's creepy feet caressing the singer's face. Adding in accusations of the tune being a "rape song"—as well as the fact that the unedited video was banned by media sources while the song itself was banished by college universities—you have yourself a bona fide #1 hit. Forgive me if this comes as a shock, but sex sells. So it wasn't exactly a thick-headed idea for Robin to combine forces with artists-and/or/maybe-producers T. I. and Pharrell Williams to create one big sex-o-rama of a track that would ooze its way all the way up to the top of the Hot 100—and just a few years before the #MeToo movement would either lock up or ostracize half of the entertainment industry.

But was "Blurred Lines" such a salacious and controversial song warranting a #1 placement? Some didn't think so. As critic Maura Johnston had noted in *The Guardian*, "It really did boggle my mind when people started freaking out about it. This is just a cheesy pickup line song and everyone was like: 'No, it's about forcing a woman against her will.' There are so many songs out there that are worse about demeaning women." Still, if much ado was being made about nothing when it came to the song's hookup lyrics, quite a bit of ruckus was resonating in regards to its music video. The "topless" version of the video (the one that was banned) created such a buzz that "Blurred Lines" could only be destined for chart-topping status. But was all this buzz enough for "Blurred Lines" to top the Hot 100 for *twelve* straight weeks in 2013?

I'm glad you asked . . .

From late June (just after Edward Snowden dumped a bunch of classified documents and *The Office* was put out of its misery like Old Yeller) until early September 2013 (right before *Grand Theft Auto 5* hit the market for some wholesome family fun), "Blurred Lines" was untouchable. All that everybody else vying for the #1 spot could do was touch themselves. The song was a nonstop hedonistic party destined for a billion YouTube clicks. But the trained listener cannot help but hear traces of Marvin Gaye's own 1977 chart-topper, "Got to Give It Up," when putting on the Robin Thicke hit. And while it's a little confusing as to why Gaye's song made such an impression on the charts back in its day, the longevity of the success of "Blurred Lines" is starting to come into focus.

"Got to Give It Up" was edited down from its time-absorbing inclusion on Gaye's two-record concert set, *Live at the London Palladium*, and not one second of its near twelve-minute time span was recorded onstage. False advertising aside, listeners still got their groove on to the jubilant, party-like atmosphere of the tune and danced it all the way to the top of the Hot 100 for one week in June 1977. As mentioned in the Hall & Oates chapter, there was quite a lot going on, musically, in the summer of that year. But people sure liked to boogie-oogie-oogie under the disco ball, therefore explaining the appeal of "Got to Give It Up."

Thirty-six years later, the groove of Gaye's "Got to Give It Up" was still infectious enough to make an impression on listeners of the digital age and undoubtedly offered a helping hand in getting "Blurred Lines" to the top of the pop chart. In fact, the late Motown legend's family estate couldn't agree with this more and would snatch up $5.3 million from Robin Thicke and his partners in crime for copyright infringement and misconduct. All the boobs and freaky feet in the world cannot compete with a groove as catchy as something created by Marvin Gaye during the '70s, and "Blurred Lines" was clearly a beneficiary of "Got to Give It Up"—it just wouldn't have done diddly doo-doo on the charts without it. So, at the end of the day, it was all worth it.

As for the song's lyrical content, it's difficult to defend a guy's pickup line involving the need to "liberate" his prey. Certainly, there are more jaw-dropping suggestions on earlier selections in this book (see "My Ding-a-ling"), but Thicke really should be ashamed by "Blurred Lines." *Really* ashamed. I just hope that before his 2016 death, actor and composer Alan Thicke had a Jason Seaver to Mike Seaver talk with his son about this questionable behavior—at least until smiles were shown again.

LIL NAS X FEATURING BILLY RAY CYRUS—
"OLD TOWN ROAD" (2019)

Payback is indeed a bitch. But sometimes payback can take a few decades to bear any fruit.

To say the music industry had gone through a paradigm shift during the first two decades of the twenty-first century would be an understatement. With physical music (at least not in vinyl format) going the way of the dinosaurs, artists—primarily of the hip-hop genre—counted on alternative media sources, including social media platforms like Facebook and Instagram, to spread their music around the world like wildfire. Going "viral" was suddenly a good thing as opposed to something you might need penicillin to treat.

The first artist who took advantage of the viral bug for substantial success on the *Billboard* charts was seventeen-year-old Soulja Boy Tell 'Em and his 2007 chart-topping hit, "Crank That (Soulja Boy)." The hip-hop artist knew exactly what he was doing by uploading the homemade single—and dance instructions for it—to YouTube for tens of millions of views, resulting in not only millions of ringtone sales but a total of seven weeks at the top of the Hot 100. Several other hip-hop artists had counted on dance crazes (2012's "Harlem Shake" by Baauer) or other trends (2016's "Black Beatles" by Rae Sremmurd [featuring Gucci Mane], which exploited the moronic Mannequin Challenge) for #1 hits. (Remember how I mentioned earlier that the Hot 100 would turn into the Wild West?)

Rapper Lil Nas X might not have relied on any dance crazes for the success of his 2019 chart-topper, "Old Town Road," but he certainly counted on the World Wide Web to get the song into the ears of the listening public. "Old Town Road"—an apparent amalgamation of hip-hop and country music—was first posted by the artist on his TikTok account in December 2018. In the months to follow, the tune would gather some major streaming credentials before the artist was signed by Columbia Records in March 2019. After strange bedfellow Billy Ray Cyrus agreed to appear on a remixed version of "Old Town Road" the following month, the tune skyrocketed to the #1 spot of the Hot 100 and remained there for nineteen straight weeks, becoming the longest-running chart-topper in the history of the Hot 100, at least at the time of this writing. To give credit where credit is due, Lil Nas X is the official #1 hit king for releasing such a history-making song.

But about that song . . .

When listening to "Old Town Road," it's clear there is nothing remotely "country" about it, aside from Billy Ray Cyrus's vocal and the mention of a horse. If the song dragged any slower, the horse in question could get so bored it might turn itself into glue. There's *got* to be something more interesting to do while "Old Town Road" is playing. (Might I suggest a can of slow-drying paint?) After its initial release, "Old Town Road" was simultaneously bubbling on the Hot 100, R&B/Hip-Hop Songs, and Country charts. But right before Cyrus had gotten involved in the track, *Billboard* had yanked the song from its Country chart. This action reportedly led to Cyrus's decision to creatively intervene. And the involvement of the country star is just the jolt "Old Town Road" needed to be on its way to Hot 100 history. The song's monstrous run at the top was indeed a matter of karma—but not in the way you'd think.

You might recall several chapters back that Billy Ray Cyrus's 1992 hit, "Achy Breaky Heart," had struggled to achieve a #1 placement on the Hot 100, peaking at #4. And if you venture back a few more chapters, you'll remember Vanessa Williams had wiped out five looooong weeks of the top spot in the spring of 1992 with "Save the Best for Last." That ballad was the biggest roadblock that kept Billy Ray and his mullet from achieving Hot 100 domination. To Cyrus, the world was indeed a crazy place.

"Achy Breaky Heart" should have given Billy Ray Cyrus a #1 hit on both the Hot 100 and Country charts in 1992 (setting aside the R&B/Hip-Hop side of things). Twenty-seven years later, the singer would have his revenge by having his name slapped on "Old Town Road." There's very little doubt that Lil Nas X worked his ass off getting his song into the cyber-sphere of music downloaders, but it was only after Cyrus put his name on it that "Old Town Road" achieved its record-breaking nineteen-week run. Does this mean Cyrus is somehow a musical dream weaver who can inflict chart success on any song he chooses? Nope. But there very well might have been a dream weaver that, after two and a half decades, did its magic and gave the achy breaky artist his due.

24KGOLDN FEATURING IANN DIOR— "MOOD" (2020)

2 4kGoldn's 2020 chart-topper, "Mood," might not be remembered for generations to come and, like "Old Town Road," it certainly counted on online exposure for its initial success. But the song has one glaring attribute that sets it apart from many of its viral contemporaries that were making noise on the charts: It's good. The catchy, melodious nature of "Mood" is a total surprise from an artist (née Golden Landis Von Jones) whose stage name is missing a vowel and some spacing. What's not terribly surprising is the fact that the single was released on major label Columbia Records (who, you will recall, had snatched up Lil Nas X on its roster). As with "Old Town Road," the suits must have known that 24kGoldn's blend of hip-hop, rock, and pop for "Mood" made for a good musical elixir, considering the not-so-inspiring material that had been lingering on the charts for the past decade.

As the story goes, 24kGoldn was hanging around his pad and playing *Call of Duty* with rapper Iann Dior (who appears on "Mood") and producers Omer Fedi and KBeaZy, although the latter two got bored with all the carnage and started coming up with some beats. While they were doing so, 24KGoldn and Dior snapped out some lyrics and hooks, and the rest is history. This incident reminds me of when Axl Rose and Slash were playing *Duck Hunt* before Slash became bored and picked up his guitar to come up with a killer lick. While Axl was still shooting the plastic gun at the TV, the singer managed to come up with the lyrics for what would become the chart-topping "Sweet Child o' Mine." (Yes, this story is completely made up.)

The opening alternative guitar pattern that kicks off "Mood" fools the listener into thinking it's a rock track, until the rattlesnake beat arrives to make it all but clear we are in hip-hop territory. Or are we? 24kGoldn and Dior don't rap the lyrics but rather sing them in an emotional manner that practically puts us all in the same room where all the complaints are being leveled at the moody girlfriend in question. "Mood," which clocks in well under the three-minute mark, is so well done that, for the year 2020, it begs the question: How did this (wonderful) shit become a #1 hit?

Were listeners thirsting for timeless songwriting as opposed to noises that follow viral trends? Was there a sea change in pop music? Was the old guard of sleazy record companies making a comeback with their smug executives—complete with cigars dangling from their mouths—telling artists and listeners what they should be listening to? Everyone who thinks any of these scenarios hold any water should socially distance themselves six feet away as to not get their N95 masks slapped off their silly faces.

By the time "Mood" was released in July 2020, all of America—and the whole world, for that matter—had experienced several months of a bad mood in the form of COVID-19 lockdowns. So when restrictions were loosening up that summer, the idea of sipping a beer in the confines of a brick-and-mortar bar—as opposed to sipping one while on a glitch-filled Zoom session—seemed awfully enticing. The same went for good music. Pop music fans (at least temporarily) welcomed a catchy ditty as opposed to a record made in the time it takes to heat up a Hot Pocket. 24kGoldn could very well have been in the right place at the right time when it came to the release of "Mood." And much like those ridiculous color-coded tiers states used to determine when bartenders and servers needed to remain at home and play *Call of Duty* (or *Duck Hunt*) rather than make a living, "Mood" fluctuated on and off the #1 spot of the Hot 100 for eight weeks from October 2020 through January 2021.

At the end of the day, good music rules. And *that's* what truly makes a song a #1 hit.

Bonus Track

BRENDA LEE–"ROCKIN' AROUND THE CHRISTMAS TREE" (2023)

Mariah Carey's Wall of Sound–inspired holiday anthem, "All I Want for Christmas Is You," has indeed become the gift that keeps on giving for decades. But the tune itself didn't top the Hot 100 until twenty-five years after its original 1994 release. Thanks to a renewed interest in the song during the 2010s—combined with massive streaming and numerous cover versions by others—"All I Want for Christmas Is You" would, for the first time, find itself inside the Top 10 in 2017, before claiming the top spot two years later. During the next three holiday seasons, the song would repeat this #1 feat.

2023 was no exception for the Carey tune, as it would once again take up the #1 position on the Hot 100 for the final two weeks of the year. But before one bar of "All I Want for Christmas" could claim this chart-topping victory, something strange happened: Brenda Lee's 1958 classic, "Rockin' Around the Christmas Tree," was resurrected and would take up the #1 spot for two weeks in early December. "All I Want for Christmas" would surely knock "Rockin' Around the Christmas Tree" off the top for its own two-week run, but Lee would strike back for chart domination for one more week in early January (supposedly for those holiday procrastinators who hadn't yet taken the trees they were rockin' around out to the gutter yet).

Brenda Lee recorded "Rockin' Around the Christmas Tree" while she was still in junior high school, but the tune wouldn't exactly deck any halls of the Hot 100 until 1960, following the considerable pop success of the young diva's trademark single, "I'm Sorry." Peaking just outside the Top 10 that year, "Rockin' Around the Christmas Tree" would gain far more notoriety for generations to come in the form of commercials, holiday TV specials, and countless films (most notably *Home Alone*, during the scene in which Kevin tries to scare off the burglars by means of puppeteering mannequins while a Michael Jordan standee moves about on a train set). But what made the Lee song—which follows the "The Chipmunk Song" and "All I Want for Christmas Is You" as the third ever Christmas single to top the Hot 100—so special in 2023?

Just like "All I Want for Christmas Is You," "Rockin' Around the Christmas Tree" counted on boatloads of streaming for its belated chart-topping success. It seems that if the interest (and streaming service) is there, the sky is certainly the limit for any song to wiggle its way to the top of the Hot 100. But this is especially true during Christmas. With the shopping season starting earlier and earlier every year, streamers and listeners are given more and more time to spread (and annoy) the world with yuletide greetings. "Rockin' Around the Christmas Tree" might have gotten some major publicity in the form of a music video produced in November 2023, but the song was merely the flavor of the year when it came to retroactive Christmas classics to play while neatly wrapped presents were being converted to heaping piles of paper under the tree.

Who knows? Maybe "Telstar" will one day make another trip down the ol' chimney for some Christmas joy.

Epilogue

THE END OF THE #1 HIT?

Is the *Billboard* Hot 100 no longer relevant? The idea that a physical Grammy Award, MTV Video Music Award, or—yes—even a *Billboard* Music Award serves a better purpose on the shelf in the Beverly Hills mansion of a performer might suggest so. But much like the music industry itself, the Hot 100 continues to evolve and, if nothing else, will forever provide a snapshot of what's hot and what's not in the everchanging world of pop music. And every now and then, the list will throw us a curveball in the form of a questionable #1 hit.

Someday, being the king of the Hot 100 hill will once again mean the world to an artist. Dethroning the #1 status of another artist's hit or merely keeping that hit from hitting the top—much like a medieval hero atop a castle, slaying a mighty dragon whose flames are lapping up at him as he makes his last stand—will again provide those spoils to the victor. As for the artist who must settle for #2, disappointment will once again endure as that artist asks, "How come *my* shit didn't become a #1 hit?" But the answer to that question shall be saved for another day.

* * * * * *

Throughout this book, I made every effort to point out why lousy chart-toppers like "Dominique" and "I'm Henry VIII, I Am" were left off the list of shame. But in addition to the fifty tracks I selected are twelve more #1 stinkers that are worth mentioning, as well as my reasoning as to why they missed the cut. Please take another trip through the past to enjoy some factoids behind the following runners-up . . . the artists of the dirty dozen can thank me later for the honorable mentions.

Johnny Preston—"Running Bear" (1960)

As noted in the "Hooked on a Feeling" chapter, Johnny Preston's "ooga-chaka"–laden chant used for his 1959 single "Running Bear" served as the template for both Jonathan King's and Blue Swede's cover versions of the 1969 B. J. Thomas hit. And, as with Blue Swede's chart-topping take on "Hooked on a Feeling," Preston managed to take the god-awful "Running Bear" to the top of the Hot 100—and for *three straight weeks*—during the early months of 1960. It would have been logical to add "Running Bear" to the list, but the track does have some memorable (albeit corny) comedic aspects to it, as is the case with "Alley Oop" and "Itsy Bitsy Teenie Weenie Yellow Polka Dot Bikini."

Jimmy Soul—"If You Wanna Be Happy" (1963)

These days, simply reciting the lyrics of singer Jimmy Soul's unchivalrous "If You Wanna Be Happy" might earn for you one of those "Keep Her in Her Place" awards the National Organization for Women had sent to Paul Anka (and perhaps a deserving kick in the balls). Soul might very well have had some problems with the ladies following the two-week chart-topping run of "If You Wanna Be Happy" in May 1963, but if you set aside the offensive lyrics (which are, at times, difficult to decipher anyway), you have yourself one hell of a catchy tune.

Kyu Sakamoto—"Sukiyaki" (1963)

It's quite amazing that a song sung entirely in Japanese—and, let's face it, released less than two decades following the end of World War II—could have topped the Hot 100 for three consecutive weeks. But that's exactly what Kyu Sakamoto's "Sukiyaki" did in June 1963. But I point to the Singing Nun's chart-topping success with the French-sung "Dominque" at the end of 1963 and Top 10 covers of "Sukiyaki" by A Taste of Honey (1981) and 4 P.M. (1994) as good reasons for washing away those tears. The tune is safe.

Jimmy Gilmer and the Fireballs—"Sugar Shack" (1963)

This cutesy pop ditty by Jimmy Gilmer and the Fireballs did five weeks' worth of damage on the Hot 100 during the fall of 1963. While "Sugar Shack" is certainly no "Love Shack," it's easy to see why a tune filled with a great amount of soluble carbohydrates would appeal to the kiddos. But five straight weeks at the #1 spot? Look no further than the cheap-sounding Hammond keyboard (played by Norman Petty) that poots along throughout the track. If it weren't for the inclusion of that instrument, "Sugar Shack" would be a sugar crash.

The Carpenters—"Top of the World" (1973)

Beating up on the Carpenters is certainly not a difficult task, yet it's hard to deny the duo's soft-rock appeal during the first half of the 1970s. Still, where exactly did a hayseed of a track—recorded by an act primarily known for providing the soundtrack to countless wedding ceremonies—fit in at the upper reaches of the pop charts in 1973? Well, a song that can keep Elton John's "Goodbye Yellow Brick Road" at the #2 spot and, decades later, find characters on *Friends* singing along with it must have made a cultural impact.

Paper Lace–"The Night Chicago Died" (1974)

If you have no recollection of reading about a monumental shoot-out between mob boss Al Capone's goons and the Chicago police, it's because the event *never happened*. (The next thing you know, someone will make a movie about Eliot Ness chucking gangsters off the top of courthouse roofs.) We can give the British-bred Paper Lace a break for not getting their facts straight, but how in the world could "The Night Chicago Died" achieve a #1 placement in the US during the 1970s? One theory is that just before the tune reached the top of the Hot 100 in August 1974, President Nixon had called it quits, leaving a stunned nation that didn't give a wobbling Weeble about what was on the charts.

B. J. Thomas–"(Hey Won't You Play) Another Somebody Done Somebody Wrong Song" (1975)

At the time, this #1 ditty by B. J. Thomas held the honor of having the longest title ever for a pop chart-topper. Sure, the tune is dopey and might be a little out of fashion for the mid-1970s (whatever that was worth), but it's far too catchy to hate. Besides, who wants to type out that long-ass title over and again for an entire chapter? There were bigger fish to fry in 1975.

Tony Orlando and Dawn– "He Don't Love You (Like I Love You)" (1975)

This cover of the 1960 Jerry Butler Top 10 hit proved to be a highly successful nugget for Tony Orlando and Dawn, as it found itself at the top of the Hot 100 following the one-week run of the B. J. Thomas hit mentioned above. (Don't worry, I won't spell it out again.) Orlando's "Tie a Yellow Ribbon Round the Ole Oak Tree"—which was seen by many as a homecoming for US troops as the Vietnam War was winding down—did escape the list, but how did such a nothingburger of a cover song like "He Don't Love You (Like I Love You)" avoid humiliation? I would just call out the song's impressive arrangement, which includes a smooth, ascending lick played by vibes and strings during the breaks. And again, there was much worse garbage from 1975 to sort through.

Styx–"Babe" (1979)

For any hardcore fans of Styx (specifically of the quintet's material penned by Tommy Shaw) who finished reading this book and screamed at the pages for its omission of the band's sole Hot 100 topper, "Babe," I'm deeply sorry. The soft-rock ballad has indeed painted Styx as a ballads band, much to the frustration of group members and fans alike. (Just ask Chicago.) But the band has historically had both a hard and soft edge, as for every "Renegade" within Styx's discography, there's a "Come Sail Away." Besides, much like its chart-topping successor, Rupert Holmes's "Escape (The Piña Colada Song)," "Babe" is simply impossible to remove from your head, much like a migraine lingering for over forty years.

Patti Austin and James Ingram–"Baby, Come to Me" (1983)

As you know, I struggled to pinpoint hits that undeservedly ascended to the #1 spot during the years 1982–1985. But one track did come awfully close: the 1983 Patti Austin–James Ingram duet, "Baby, Come to Me" (which was referenced in the "There'll Be Sad Songs [To Make You Cry]" chapter). During the same year in which '80s standards like Men at Work's "Down Under" and Michael Jackson's "Beat It" were taking turns snatching the top placement of the Hot 100, it's strange to think that a weary ballad could even crack the Top 10 let alone scale to the top. But with some help from its inclusion in *General Hospital*—and, not to mention, Ingram's blaring "Hey!" heard at the final chorus (as if the singer just caught listeners snoozing)—"Baby, Come to Me" had earned its wings.

Vanilla Ice–"Ice Ice Baby" (1990)

This is the third time I'm mentioning Vanilla Ice and his Queen-killing signature song. While I'm at it, I may as well repeat the fact that "Ice Ice Baby" was the first hip-hop track to hit the top of the Hot 100. (Sorry, it just can't be undone.) But laugh all you want at Mr. Ice and all the kids who shaved lines into their hair, asked their moms to buy them the *To the Extreme* CD, and went to see *Cool as Ice* (or even *Teenage Mutant Ninja Turtles II: The Secret of the Ooze*); the marketing blitz the artist—and Snow, for that matter—put on at the dawn of the '90s was pure genius (as short-lived as it was).

Carolina Gaitán, Mauro Castillo, Adassa, Rhenzy Feliz, Diane Guerrero, Stephanie Beatriz, and the *Encanto* cast– "We Don't Talk About Bruno" (2022)

One common trait many modern #1 hits seem to share is the fact that the tunes themselves seem to promote the artists as opposed to the other way around. And with songs sales being so negligible and no longer providing a viable income for artists, the lack of energy put into the studio sessions for many of these hits makes perfect sense. And that's why the exuberant, theatrical "We Don't Talk About Bruno"—from the 2021 Disney flick *Encanto*—stuck out like a sore thumb when it topped the Hot 100 in February 2022 for five straight weeks. With 1993's "A Whole New World" being the last Disney tune to hit the #1 spot before this one managed to do so, it seemed like the days of the Mouse having any impact on the pop charts were long gone. But never forget: Even the brats enjoy listening to records. Therefore, I chose not to talk about not talking about Bruno.

You Like Me!

Thanks to Mom, Dad, Deanna, Clinton, Suzanna, Collin, David, Elaine, Mona, Pete, Shelly, Grace, Tamara, Christy, John, Andrea, and anyone else who was forced to hear about any of my harebrained book ideas.

Extra special thanks to Aaron, Eric, Jared, Kazuo, Micah, Ross, Scott, and Todd for the feedback on the cover.

Extra, extra special thanks to Marguerite and everyone at Alyce Zawacki Law, PLLC.

And an extra, extra, extra special thanks to Shilah and the crew at Bublish.

Selected Bibliography

Aguilera, Tere. "Mocedades Returns with a New 'Eres Tú', Featuring Plácido Domingo." *Billboard*, January 27, 2023. https://www.billboard.com/music/latin/mocedades-interview-eres-tu-placido-domingo-1235206476/.

Amende, Coral. *Rock Confidential: A Backstage Pass to the Outrageous World of Rock 'n' Roll*. Plume, 2000.

Ankeny, Jason. "John Denver Biography." AllMusic (accessed 2024). https://www.allmusic.com/artist/john-denver-mn0000811622.

Barendregt, Erwin. "Sly Stone's Masterpiece There's a Riot Goin' On." *A Pop Life*, November 22, 2021. https://en.apoplife.nl/sly-stones-masterpiece-theres-a-riot-goin-on/.

Bayles, Rick. "Versions: "Ol' 55." *Americana UK*, August 25, 2023. https://americana-uk.com/versions-ol-55.

The Beatles Bible. "Wino Junko." https://www.beatlesbible.com/people/paul-mccartney/songs/wino-junko/#google_vignette.

Ben. Directed by Phil Karlson. Cinerama Releasing Corporation, 1972.

Bickhart, Jim. "Watching Bobby Grow—A Decade of Hits." *Billboard*, October 5, 1974.

BillboardGuy. "30 Years Ago, The Billboard Hot 100 Singles Were Forever Changed By Broadcast Data Systems and SoundScan." November 23, 2021. https://billboardchartrewind.wordpress.com/author/billboardguy/.

Box Office Mojo. "Charlie's Angels (2000)" (accessed 2024). https://www.boxofficemojo.com/title/tt0160127/.

Breihan, Tom. "The Number Ones: All-4-One's 'I Swear.'" *Stereogum*, March 4, 2022. https://www.stereogum. com/2178175/the-number-ones-all-4-ones-i-swear/ columns/the-number-ones/.

Breihan, Tom. "The Number Ones: Lorne Greene's 'Ringo.'" *Stereogum*, July 6, 2018. https://www.stereogum.com/ 2004500/the-number-ones-lorne-greenes-ringo/columns/ the-number-ones/.

Breihan, Tom. "The Number Ones: Snow's 'Informer.'" *Stereogum*, February 2, 2022. https://www.stereogum. com/2174418/the-number-ones-snows-informer/columns/ the-number-ones/.

Breihan, Tom. "The Number Ones: Stars On 45's 'Stars On 45.'" *Stereogum*, May 8, 2020. https://www.stereogum. com/2083548/the-number-ones-stars-on-45s-stars-on-45/ columns/the-number-ones/.

Breihan, Tom. *The Number Ones: Twenty Chart-Topping Hits That Reveal the History of Pop Music.* Hachette Books, 2022.

Brokaw, Tom. "Perspectives." *Newsweek.* Special Edition: *The Winner Is . . .* 2000.

Bronson, Fred. "(You're) Having My Baby." *Super Seventies* (originally published 1988). https://www.superseventies. com/sw_yourehavingmybaby.html.

Browne, David, Jon Dolan, Kory Grow, Christopher R. Weingarten. "Best of My Love." *Rolling Stone.* Special Edition: *Eagles: The Ultimate Guide.* 2016.

Buskin, Richard. "Classic Tracks: Billy Swan 'I Can Help'." Sound on Sound, November 2007. https://www.soundonsound. com/techniques/classic-tracks-billy-swan-can-help#:~:- text=%22People%20just%20loved%20recording%20 there,Memphis%20session%20musician%20Bobby%20 Emmons.

Campbell, Courtney. "'Before the Next Teardrop Falls': The Story Behind Freddy Fender's Crossover Smash." *Wide Open Country*, June 5, 2022. https://www.wideopencountry.com/before-the-next-teardrop-falls/.

Classic Albums: Elton John—Goodbye Yellow Brick Road. Directed by Bob Smeaton. Eagle Eye Media, 2001.

Cohn, Nik. "The Fab Four." *Life*. Special Edition: *The Beatles: from Yesterday to Today*. 1995.

Crowe, Cameron. "Across the Border." *Rolling Stone*. Special Edition: *Eagles: The Ultimate Guide*. 2016.

DeRiso, Nick. "45 Years Ago: Hall and Oates Notch Their First No. 1 With 'Rich Girl.'" Ultimate Classic Rock, January 24, 2022. https://ultimateclassicrock.com/hall-and-oates-rich-girl/.

DeRiso, Nick. "45 Years Ago: Why Wings Struggled With 'Listen to What the Man Said.'" Ultimate Classic Rock, May 16, 2020. https://ultimateclassicrock.com/paul-mccartney-wings-listen-to-what-the-man-said/.

DeRiso, Nick. "Hall & Oates' 'Rich Girl' Wasn't About a Girl." Ultimate Classic Rock, February 21, 2014. https://ultimateclassicrock.com/hall-oates-rich-girl-wasnt-about-a-girl/

Discogs. "Jody Pijper" (accessed 2024). https://www.discogs.com/artist/310579-Jody-Pijper.

Dowdling, William J. *Beatlesongs*. Simon & Schuster, 1989.

Eames, Tom. "Tammi Terrell: The Tragic Life Story of a Motown Singer and How Marvin Gaye Never Got Over Her Death." *Smooth Radio*, July 21, 2020. https://www.smoothradio.com/news/music/tammi-terrell-songs-death-children-age/.

Eames, Tom. "The Story of . . . 'Amazed' by Lonestar." *Smooth Radio*, June 15, 2023. https://www.smoothradio.com/features/the-story-of/lonestar-amazed-lyrics-meaning-video-facts/.

Erlewine, Steven Thomas. "Wings Biography." AllMusic (accessed 2024). https://www.allmusic.com/artist/wings-mn0000956707.

Fandom. "ShowBiz Pizza Place" (accessed 2024). https://showbizpizza.fandom.com/wiki/ShowBiz_Pizza_Place.

Ferrier, Aimee. "The One Line John Lennon Would Use to Cheer Up the Beatles." *Far Out Magazine,* March 7, 2023. https://faroutmagazine.co.uk/line-john-lennon-used-to-cheer-up-the-beatles/.

Frey, Glenn and Don Henley. Liner notes, *Eagles—The Very Best of.* CD Booklet. Warner Music Group, 2003.

Frommer, Fred. "How the 1970s US Energy Crisis Drove Innovation." *History,* October 17, 2022. https://www.history.com/news/energy-crisis-1970s-innovation.

Galloway, A. Scott. Liner notes, *Chicago X.* CD Booklet. Warner Strategic Marketing, 2003.

Gay, Roxane. "Fifty Years Ago, Protesters Took on the Miss America Pageant and Electrified the Feminist Movement." *Smithsonian Magazine,* January 2018. https://www.smithsonianmag.com/history/fifty-years-ago-protestors-took-on-miss-america-pageant-electrified-feminist-movement-180967504/.

Graff, Gary. "How Huey Lewis Scored a Surprise Hit with 'Jacob's Ladder.'" Ultimate Classic Rock. March, 14, 2022. https://ultimateclassicrock.com/huey-lewis-jacobs-ladder/.

Grein, Paul. Liner notes, *Super Hits of the '70s, Vol. 17.* CD booklet. Rhino Records, 1993.

Hartman, Kent. *The Wrecking Crew: The Inside Story of Rock and Roll's Best-Kept Secret.* St. Martin's Press, 2012.

Hawley, Larry. "Disco Demolition Night: How an anti-disco baseball night led to a riot in Comiskey Park." *WGNTV,* July 12, 2022. https://wgntv.com/news/wgn-news-now/disco-demolition-night-how-an-anti-disco-baseball-night-led-to-a-riot-in-comiskey-park/.

Hepworth, David. *Never a Dull Moment: 1971 The Year That Rock Exploded.* Henry Holt and Company, 2016.

Hudak, Joseph. "Country Songwriter Tom T. Hall's Death Ruled a Suicide." *Rolling Stone,* January 5, 2022. https://www.

rollingstone.com/music/music-country/tom-t-hall-suicide-cause-of-death-1278971/.

Huey, Steve. "Billy Swan Biography." AllMusic (accessed 2024). https://www.allmusic.com/artist/billy-swan-mn0000768584 #biography.

Hunter, Glenn. "Fifty-five Years Later, the Harper Valley P.T.A. Is Still in Session." *Texas Monthly*, November 2, 2022. https://www.texasmonthly.com/arts-entertainment/jeannie-c-riley-on-harper-valley-pta-song/.

Jackson, Andrew Grant. *1973: Rock at the Crossroads*. Thomas Dunne Books, 2019.

Johns, Glyn. *Sound Man: A Life Recording Hits with The Rolling Stones, The Who, Led Zeppelin, the Eagles, Eric Clapton, the Faces . . .* Plume, 2014.

Jones, Abby. "It's 'Alright': How Kenny Loggins Helped Change Music in Film With 'Caddyshack.'" *Billboard*, April 24, 2018. https://www.billboard.com/culture/tv-film/caddyshack-kenny-loggins-music-in-film-8377024/.

Joseph, Ben. *Chicago: Feelin' Stronger Every Day*. Quarry Press, 2000.

Kellman, Andy. "Sweet Sensation Biography." AllMusic (accessed 2024). https://www.allmusic.com/artist/sweet-sensation-mn0000048507

Lambert, Arden. "Bobby Goldsboro's 'Honey' Was Named the Worst Song Ever! Here's Why." *Country Thang Daily*, August 20, 2020. https://www.countrythangdaily.com/honey-bobby-goldsboro/.

Leahey, Andrew. "Maroon 5 Biography." AllMusic (accessed 2024). https://www.allmusic.com/artist/maroon-5-mn0000285232 #biography.

Leepson, Marc. "Barry Sadler: American Soldier, Songwriter, and Author." *Britannica*, May 9, 2024 (updated). https://www.britannica.com/biography/Barry-Sadler.

Levy, Michael. "United States Presidential Election of 2000." *Britannica*, November 1, 2024. (updated) https://www.britannica.com/event/United-States-presidential-election-of-2000.

Lundy, Zeth. *Stevie Wonder's Songs in the Key of Life (33 1/3)*. Continuum, 2007.

Lynskey, Dorian. "Blurred Lines: The Most Controversial Song of the Decade." *The Guardian*, November 13, 2013. https://www.theguardian.com/music/2013/nov/13/blurred-lines-most-controversial-song-decade.

Married With Children. "Oldies But Young 'Uns," Season 5, Episode 17. Fox. Air date: March 17, 1991.

Marsh, David. *Louie Louie: The History and Mythology of the World's Most Famous Rock 'N' Roll Song*. Hyperion, 1993.

Matos, Michaelangelo. "How SoundScan Changed Music, Driving Metal, Rap and Alt-Rock Up the Charts." *Billboard*, June 10, 2021. https://www.billboard.com/pro/how-soundscan-changed-music-charts-success/.

Matthews, Tom. "A Year in History: Timeline of 1969 Events." Historic Newspapers (updated), December 15, 2021. https://www.historic-newspapers.co.uk/blog/a-year-in-history-timeline-of-1969-events/.

Molanphy, Chris. "How The Hot 100 Became America's Hit Barometer." NPR, August 1, 2013. https://www.npr.org/sections/therecord/2013/08/16/207879695/how-the-hot-100-became-americas-hit-barometer.

Newman, Randy. Liner notes, *Guilty: 30 Years of Randy Newman*. CD booklet. Rhino Entertainment Company, 1998.

Nights With Alice Cooper. "Flashback: Pink Floyd's 'Another Brick in the Wall (Part 2)' Tops the Charts." March 22, 2022. https://nightswithalicecooper.com/2022/03/22/flashback-pink-floyds-another-brick-in-the-wall-part-2-tops-the-charts/#:~:text=It%20was%2042%20years%20ago,100%20charts%20for%20four%20weeks.

O'Brien, Andrew. "John Lennon Gives His Final Live Performance, With Elton John at MSG, On This Day In '74." *Live For Live Music*, November 28, 2023. https://liveforlivemusic.com/features/john-lennon-elton-john-final-performance/.

O'Rourke, Sally. "It Was 50 Years Ago Today: 'Winchester Cathedral' by The New Vaudeville Band." *Rebeat*, 2016. https://www.rebeatmag.com/it-was-50-years-ago-today-winchester-cathedral-by-the-new-vaudeville-band.

Onion, Amanda, Matt Mullen, Missy Sullivan, and Christian Zapata. "December 21, 2012." *History* (updated), August 21, 2018. https://www.history.com/topics/religion/december-21-2012.

Onion, Amanda, Matt Mullen, Missy Sullivan, and Christian Zapata. "'The Macarena' Begins Its Reign atop the U.S. Pop Charts.'" *History* (accessed 2024). https://www.history.com/this-day-in-history/the-macarena-begins-its-reign-atop-the-u-s-pop-charts.

Onion, Amanda, Matt Mullen, Missy Sullivan, and Christian Zapata. "Staff Sergeant Barry Sadler hits #1 with "Ballad of the Green Berets." *History* (accessed 2024). https://www.history.com/this-day-in-history/staff-sergeant-barry-sadler-hits-1-with-ballad-of-the-green-berets.

Patton, Alli. "Who is the Songwriter Behind the Johnny Carson Theme Song?" American Songwriter, 2023. https://americansongwriter.com/who-is-the-songwriter-behind-the-johnny-carson-theme-song/.

Pennington, Susan. "Oscars Flashback 50 Years Ago to 1974: Streaker Shows 'His Shortcomings' During Memorable Ceremony." *Gold Derby*, March 4, 2024. https://www.goldderby.com/feature/oscars-flashback-1974-streaker-1205756200/.

Pitts Jr., Leonard. Liner notes, *Stevie Wonder: At the Turn of a Century*. CD Booklet. Motown, 1999.

Planer, Lindsay. "Rock of the Westies Review." AllMusic (accessed 2024). https://www.allmusic.com/album/rock-of-the-westies-mw0000194371.

Rutherford, Kevin. "Rewinding the Charts: In 1972, Chuck Berry Took His 'Ding-a-Ling' to No. 1." *Billboard*, October 21, 2017. https://www.billboard.com/pro/chuck-berry-my-ding-a-ling-rewinding-the-charts-1972/.

Sales, Michael. "Phil Collins Goes Train Robbing in the Midlands." *Midlands Movies*, June 16, 2020. https://www.midlands-movies.com/phil-collins-goes-train-robbing-in-the-midlands.

Sanchez, Tony. *Up and Down with the Rolling Stones*. Signet, 1979.

Selvin, Joel. "BEST OF THE BEATLES / 'Anthology' pulls together rare photos and in-depth interviews with band members." *SFGATE*, October 4, 2000. https://www.sfgate.com/music/article/best-of-the-beatles-anthology-pulls-together-3303015.php.

Seraphine, Danny. *Street Player: My Chicago Story*. John Wiley & Sons, 2010.

Setlist.fm. "Lanchester Arts Festival 1972 Setlists" (accessed 2024). https://www.setlist.fm/festival/1972/lanchester-arts-festival-1972-6bd6861e.html.

Songfacts. Selected articles:

— "'Mr. Custer' by Larry Verne" (accessed 2024). https://www.songfacts.com/facts/larry-verne/mr-custer.

— "'This Diamond Ring' by Gary Lewis & the Playboys" (accessed 2024). https://www.songfacts.com/facts/gary-lewis-the-playboys/this-diamond-ring.

— "'Hang On Sloopy' by the McCoys" (accessed 2024). https://www.songfacts.com/facts/the-mccoys/hang-on-sloopy.

— "'The Ballad of The Green Berets' by Staff Sergeant Barry Sadler" (accessed 2024). https://www.song-facts.com/facts/staff-sergeant-barry-sadler/the-ballad-of-the-green-berets.

— "'Winchester Cathedral' by New Vaudeville Band" (accessed 2024). https://www.songfacts.com/facts/new-vaudeville-band/winchester-cathedral.

— "'Honey' by Bobby Goldsboro" (accessed 2024). https://www.songfacts.com/facts/bobby-goldsboro/honey.

— "'Harper Valley P.T.A.' by Jeannie C. Riley" (accessed 2024). https://www.songfacts.com/facts/jeannie-c-riley/harper-valley-pta.

— "'Ode To Billie Joe' by Bobbie Gentry" (accessed 2024). https://www.songfacts.com/facts/bobbie-gentry/ode-to-billie-joe.

— "'Sugar, Sugar' by The Archies" (accessed 2024). https://www.songfacts.com/facts/the-archies/sugar-sugar.

— "'Mama Told Me (Not to Come)' by Three Dog Night" (accessed 2024). https://www.songfacts.com/facts/three-dog-night/mama-told-me-not-to-come.

— "'Ain't No Mountain High Enough' by Diana Ross" (accessed 2024). https://www.songfacts.com/facts/diana-ross/aint-no-mountain-high-enough.

— "'Family Affair' by Sly & the Family Stone" (accessed 2024). https://www.songfacts.com/facts/sly-the-family-stone/family-affair.

— "'Ben' by Michael Jackson" (accessed 2024). https://www.songfacts.com/facts/michael-jackson/ben.

— "'One Bad Apple' by the Osmonds" (accessed 2024). https://www.songfacts.com/facts/the-osmonds/one-bad-apple.

— "'My Ding-a-Ling' by Chuck Berry" (accessed 2024). https://www.songfacts.com/facts/chuck-berry/my-ding-a-ling.

— "'Angie' by The Rolling Stones" (accessed 2024). https://www.songfacts.com/facts/the-rolling-stones/angie.

— "'You're Sixteen' by Ringo Starr" (accessed 2024). https://www.songfacts.com/facts/ringo-starr/youre-sixteen.

— "'Hooked On a Feeling' by B. J. Thomas" (accessed 2024). https://www.songfacts.com/facts/bj-thomas/hooked-on-a-feeling.

— "'(You're) Having My Baby' by Paul Anka" (accessed 2024). https://www.songfacts.com/facts/paul-anka/youre-having-my-baby.

— "'You Haven't Done Nothin'' by Stevie Wonder" (accessed 2024). https://www.songfacts.com/facts/stevie-wonder/you-havent-done-nothin.

— "'I Can Help' by Billy Swan" (accessed 2024). https://www.songfacts.com/facts/billy-swan/i-can-help.

— "'Please Mr. Postman' by the Marvelettes" (accessed 2024). https://www.songfacts.com/facts/the-marvelettes/please-mr-postman.

— "'Before the Next Teardrop Falls' by Freddy Fender" (accessed 2024). https://www.songfacts.com/facts/freddy-fender/before-the-next-teardrop-falls.

— "'Island Girl' by Elton John" (accessed 2024). https://www.songfacts.com/facts/elton-john/island-girl.

— "'Another Brick in The Wall (Part 2)' by Pink Floyd" (accessed 2024). https://www.songfacts.com/facts/pink-floyd/another-brick-in-the-wall-part-ii.

— "'Stars On 45 Medley' by Stars on 45" (accessed 2024). https://www.songfacts.com/facts/stars-on-45/stars-on-45-medley.

— "'There'll Be Sad Songs (To Make You Cry)' by Billy Ocean" (accessed 2024). https://www.song-facts.com/facts/billy-ocean/therell-be-sad-songs-to-make-you-cry.

— "'Amanda' by Boston" (accessed 2024). https://www.songfacts.com/facts/boston/amanda.

— "'Jacob's Ladder' by Huey Lewis & the News" (accessed 2024). https://www.songfacts.com/facts/huey-lewis-the-news/jacobs-ladder.

— "'You Keep Me Hangin' On' by the Supremes" (accessed 2024). https://www.songfacts.com/facts/the-supremes/you-keep-me-hangin-on.

— "'Rock On' by David Essex" (accessed 2024). https://www.songfacts.com/facts/david-essex/rock-on.

— "'To Be with You' by Mr. Big" (accessed 2024). https://www.songfacts.com/facts/mr-big/to-be-with-you.

— "'Informer' by Snow" (accessed 2024). https://www.songfacts.com/facts/snow/informer.

— "'Macarena' by Los del Rio" (accessed 2024). https://www.songfacts.com/facts/los-del-rio/macarena.

— "'Wild Wild West' by Will Smith" (accessed 2024). https://www.songfacts.com/facts/will-smith/wild-wild-west.

— "'Amazed' by Lonestar" (accessed 2024). https://www.songfacts.com/facts/lonestar/amazed.

— "'Independent Women Part 1' by Destiny's Child" (accessed 2024). https://www.songfacts.com/facts/destinys-child/independent-women-part-i.

— "'You're Beautiful' by James Blunt" (accessed 2024). https://www.songfacts.com/facts/james-blunt/youre-beautiful.

— "'One More Night by Maroon 5" (accessed 2024). https://www.songfacts.com/facts/maroon-5/one-more-night.

— "'Blurred Lines' by Robin Thicke" (accessed 2024). https://www.songfacts.com/facts/robin-thicke/blurred-lines.

— "'Old Town Road' by Lil Nas X" (accessed 2025). https://www.songfacts.com/facts/lil-nas-x/old-town-road.

— "'Mood' by 24kGoldn" (accessed 2024). https://www.songfacts.com/facts/24kgoldn/mood.

— "'Rockin' Around the Christmas Tree' by Brenda Lee" (accessed 2024). https://www.songfacts.com/facts/brenda-lee/rockin-around-the-christmas-tree.

— "'All I Want for Christmas Is You' by Mariah Carey" (accessed 2024). https://www.songfacts.com/facts/mariah-carey/all-i-want-for-christmas-is-you.

Southpark.cc. "Cat Orgy" (accessed 2024). https://southpark.cc.com/w/index.php/Cat_Orgy.

Southpark.cc. "Two Guy Naked in a Hot Tub" (accessed 2024). https://southpark.cc.com/wiki/Two_Guys_Naked_in_a_Hot_Tub.

Springer, Matt. "How Elton John Scaled Back on 'Rock of the Westies.'" Ultimate Classic Rock, October 24, 2015. https://ultimateclassicrock.com/elton-john-rock-of-the-westies/.

Tamarkin, Jeff. "Barry McGuire vs. Barry Sadler: When the News Hit #1." Best Classic Bands (accessed 2024). https://bestclassicbands.com/barry-mcguire-sadler-green-berets-12-7-188/.

Taupin, Bernie. *Scattershot: Life, Music, Elton, and Me*. Hachette Books, 2023.

Taylor, Tom. "The Little-known Song That Johnny Cash Ripped Off for 'Folsom Prison Blues.'" Far Out Magazine. September 5, 2023. https://faroutmagazine.co.uk/the-little-known-song-that-johnny-cash-ripped-off-for-folsom-prison-blues/

Tsioulcas, Anastasia. "The Life and Death Of Tower Records, Revisited." NPR, October 15, 2015. https://www.npr.org/sections/therecord/2015/10/20/450038047/the-life-and-death-of-tower-records-revisited.

Walthall, Catherine. "The Story Behind the One-Hit Wonder 'Hooked on a Feeling' by Blue Swede." *American Songwriter*,

2022. https://americansongwriter.com/the-story-behind-the-one-hit-wonder-hooked-on-a-feeling-by-blue-swede/.

Ward, Ed. "The Woodstock Music and Art Fair." *Britannica* (accessed 2024). https://www.britannica.com/topic/The-Woodstock-Music-and-Art-Fair-1688509.

Wardlaw, Matt. "30 Years Ago: Mr. Big's Life-Changing 'To Be with You' Hits No. 1.'" Ultimate Classic Rock, February 28, 2022. https://ultimateclassicrock.com/mr-big-to-be-with-you-number-one/.

Wayte, Larry. *Pay for Play: How the Music Industry Works, Where the Money Goes, and Why.* University of Oregon/ Pressbooks, 2023.

Welch, Chris. Liner notes, *Telstar: The Complete Tornados.* CD booklet. Repertoire Records, 1998.

Westerman, Ashley. "50 Years Later, the Archies' 'Sugar, Sugar' Is Still 'Really Sweet'." NPR, September 20, 2019. https:// www.npr.org/2019/09/20/761616330/50-years-later-the-archies-sugar-sugar-is-still-really-sweet.

Wikipedia. "1 (Beatles album)" (accessed 2024). https://en.wikipedia.org/wiki/1_(Beatles_album)#cite_note-decade-3.

Wikipedia. "Billboard Hot 100" (accessed 2024). https://en.wikipedia.org/wiki/Billboard_Hot_100.

Wikipedia. "Lists of Billboard Number-One Singles" (accessed 2024). https://en.wikipedia.org/wiki/Lists_of_Billboard_number-one_singles.

Wikipedia. "Lonestar Discography" (accessed 2024). https:// en.wikipedia.org/wiki/Lonestar_discography.

Wood, Jay. "The History of Music Charts: From Sheet Music to Digital Streaming." *New Music World*, March 22, 2023. https://newmusicworld.org/history-of-music-charts/.

The Wrecking Crew! DVD. Directed by Denny Tedesco. Magnolia Home Entertainment, 2015.

"Macarena" (Bayside Boys Mix) © 1995 by Sony Music Entertainment España, S.L.

"Wild Wild West" © 1999 by Sony Music Entertainment Inc. and Overbrook Music LLC

"Amazed" © 1999 by Sony Music Entertainment and BMG Entertainment

"Independent Women" © 2000 by Columbia Records, a division of Sony Music Entertainment

"You're Beautiful" © 2004 by Atlantic Recording Corporation

"One More Night" © 2012 by Interscope Records

"Blurred Lines" © 2013 by I Like 'Em Thicke Music, More Water from Nazareth Publishing Inc., Sony/ATV Allegro, Deyjah's Daddy Muzik, and EMI Pop Music Publishing

"Old Town Road" © 2018 by Form and Texture Inc., Songs of Universal Inc., Sony/ATV Songs LLC, and Songs in the Key of Mink

"Mood" © 2020 by Columbia Records, KBeaZy, Blake Slatkin, Iann Dior, Omer Fedi, and 24kGoldn

"Rockin' Around the Christmas Tree" © 1958 by St. Nicholas Music Inc. and UMG Recordings, Inc.

"Running Bear" © 2021 by Universal Digital Enterprises

"If You Wanna Be Happy" © 1963 by BMG Gold Songs

"Sukiyaki" © 1961 by Sony Music Publishing Inc. (and Sony/ATV Songs LLC)

"Sugar Shack" © 1963 by Universal Music Group

"Top of the World" © 1972 by Almo Music Corp.

"The Night Chicago Died" © 1974 by Mercury Records Limited, Dance Plant Records (2012)

"(Hey Won't You Play) Another Somebody Done Somebody Wrong Song" © 1975 by Universal Music Group

"He Don't Love You (Like I Love You)" © 1975 by Elektra Records

"Babe" © 1979 by A&M Records Inc., Stygian Songs, and Almo Music Corp.

"Baby, Come to Me" © 1981 by UMG Recordings, Inc.

Opening Quotes

Will Smith: *60 Minutes*. Interview. CBS. Originally broadcast on December 2, 2007.

Joe Elliott: Hyden, Stephen. Interview. *A.V. Club*. July 20, 2011.

Kathy Valentine: *AZQuotes.com*. Retrieved August 21, 2024, from AZQuotes.com: https://www.azquotes.com/quote/785435.

Mel Tormé: Tomkins, Les. Interview. 1976.

Sting: VH1 TV Promo, 1991.

www.ingramcontent.com/pod-product-compliance
Lightning Source LLC
Chambersburg PA
CBHW071553210326
41597CB00019B/3229